# A
# MOTHER'S
# JOB

# A MOTHER'S JOB

## JOY DOVE

### *with* SUNDAY TIMES BESTSELLING AUTHORS ANN and JOE CUSACK

MIRROR BOOKS

m
B

MIRROR BOOKS

1

Published in Great Britain and Ireland in 2022 by
Mirror Books, a Reach PLC business.

www.mirrorbooks.co.uk
@TheMirrorBooks

Print ISBN 9781915306159
eBook ISBN 9781915306166

Edited by Harri Aston
Page design and typesetting by Danny Lyle

Printed and bound in Great Britain by
CPI Group (UK) Ltd, Croydon, CR0 4YY

I would like to dedicate my book to my beloved Jodey, and to all those who have helped me on my journey for justice.

# PROLOGUE
# SEPTEMBER 2019

As my cab pulled up outside the hotel, I stared, astonished, out of the window. I had never seen so many police officers and security workers in my entire life. There was even a doorman with a black top hat and a bow tie.

"They'll never let me in," I gasped, almost to myself.

All the way down here, on the train, I'd been swept along on a wave of adrenaline, scribbling down the finishing touches to my speech, ready and impatient to tell the Labour Party conference about my Jodey.

But now that I was here, at the Grand Hotel, Brighton, I felt suddenly insignificant and incidental, as though I had physically shrunk. I wasn't at all sure I'd get past this long watchful line of policemen. The tension seemed to ripple through each officer like an electric current, ready to shock me if I dared to approach.

After all, who was I? A pensioner from Stockton-on-Tees. An anonymous little old lady. I had never given a speech in my entire life. I'd never so much as addressed the local knitting club, never mind a national political conference.

I could taste the tang of sea salt in the air as I stepped out of the taxi and in that moment, I was back in 1980, on the beach with a six-year-old Jodey, her sandy fingers curled around mine, her pockets full of shells and shiny pebbles. Her pockets full of plans, hopes and dreams.

*Nobody should die like that.*

Incredibly, I was waved past the police officers, through the main entrance, but my anxiety only thickened and fogged. It was only the thought of my Jodey, of her bone-deep desperation in those last lonely hours, that drove me forwards.

Waiting in the queue to have my bag searched, I spotted Labour leader Jeremy Corbyn, Keir Starmer [then the party's Brexit spokesman] and Ken Livingstone [former London mayor] and I felt my stomach plunging. Here I was, in my £2 charity shop blouse and grey trousers. They had felt like such a bargain. Now, they felt inadequate, embarrassing. I was an imposter.

*Could I really do this?*

"Your bag please," said a security worker, and, as I handed it over, I suddenly remembered the egg and cress sandwiches I'd packed for the train yesterday, untouched, and doubtless by now rancid and festering at the bottom of my bag.

The notion was both mortifying and hilarious, and I imagined Jodey next to me, snorting with laughter, leaning in to give me a playful hug and a dig in the ribs. Her ghost was so present, I could almost catch a glimpse of her fair hair as the autumn sunlight streamed through the Victorian windows.

Typical of you, Mam. We can't take you anywhere! You'll knock the poor fella sick when he gets a whiff of those butties. Despite myself, I giggled, and the tension seemed to slide out me, displaced instead by a steely sense of purpose and pride. I was growing taller, stronger. My resolve was granite.

Nobody in authority had cared about Jodey when she was alive. Now that it was too late, they were falling over themselves to apologise. Falling over themselves to keep me quiet.

There was nothing special about me; and that was exactly why I had to make this speech and make my voice heard.

I walked through the great hall and into the packed conference room, marching onto the podium as though I owned the place, at once out of my depth yet completely at ease.

I left my speech folded in the pocket of my bargain trousers and instead, the words flowed, straight from my heart.

"My Jodey was treated shamefully," I said firmly. "She took her own life after having her benefits stopped.

"A letter arrived from the DWP saying she was fit to work. By then, she was at the undertakers."

I'd brought along some photos to show at the conference; Jodey's first day at school, Jodey's wedding, Jodey's first child...the happiness shone out of her... then, Jodey's grave, Jodey's post-mortem report...

As I drew breath, and looked out across the sea of faces, I saw many wiping away tears, many getting to their feet in ovation. My own cheeks were wet with emotion. And pride. My voice rang out over the applause; clear and self-assured:

"As a mother I will never give up this fight for justice."

# 1
# Lucky Girl

JUNE 1981

Scanning the kitchen worktops again, I tutted and shook my head. Was I losing my memory? I could have sworn there was almost half a chocolate cake left after dinner. But now there was no sign of the cake tin or, for that matter, the cake itself.

As I searched around the kitchen, a little voice floated through the open window from the back garden.

"Eat up dollies, come on! Yummy chocolate cake!"

Suppressing a laugh, I marched out through the back door to find my six-year-old daughter, Jodey, with her line of dollies – Sarah, Tracey and Susan – propped up against the garden fence. They all – Jodey included – had tell-tale smears of chocolate across their faces. Jodey's wavy brown hair was pulled back into a ponytail, and she was wearing a bright pink T-shirt and orange shorts, with her hands and knees covered in a fetching mixture of mud and cake. As she turned towards me, I was struck, as always, by the dazzling sapphire blue of her eyes.

"We're having a picnic," she explained brightly. "Sit down, Mam, I've saved you a slice, only a little one, mind."

"That's extremely generous of you," I said drily, but Jodey didn't seem to notice. She was too busy spooning more cake into Sarah's mouth, which of course fell straight back out and onto her dress.

"Mam, can you wash my dollies' clothes after the picnic?" Jodey asked. "I don't know why they keep spitting this cake out."

There was no point arguing with her. I just had to admit defeat and nod along. Once my Jodey had set her heart on something, she was a real force to be reckoned with, and her life revolved around those baby dolls. Even then, as a scrap of a girl, I could see the future mother in her. The way she wiped their mouths so tenderly and sponged the stains from their dresses; it pulled at my heartstrings. There was a maternal instinct in Jodey, stronger even than my own.

"You're doing a grand job with those dolls," I told her, as I stood up ready to go back inside. "Here, you have my slice, pet."

I could still hear her chatting as I went back into the kitchen, and I shook my head and giggled. She was a real character all right, our Jodey. She was one on her own.

* * *

Jodey's dad, Eric, and I had met in 1969, when I was aged 15. I had left school early and was working in a food factory, wrapping oranges, pricing bacon, packing biscuits. There was a good bunch of girls on the line, and I liked the job, though it was long hours and poor pay. But then a pal told me of a job advertised in a local butcher's shop, better money and probably shorter hours too, I reckoned. Back then, jobs were plentiful and easy to come by; I thought nothing of giving in my notice at the factory and calling in at the butcher's on my way home. If that didn't work out, there was surely another job waiting round the corner. Chopping liver behind the counter, there was a teenage boy, around my age. He had shoulder length brown hair, which I rather liked, and he wore a white overall with a few too many bloodstains on the front.

"I believe you've a job going?" I asked with a hesitant smile.

He nodded and I noticed he blushed too, which must have been somehow infectious, because then I felt myself blushing in return. We stood awkwardly; I was fixated on the bloodstained apron and he gazed down at the liver. Neither of us seemed to know what to say next. Luckily, the boss then appeared from the back room, wiping his hands on a towel.

"You're here for the position?" he asked. "Can you start straightaway?"

I nodded my replies to every question, and that was that. I was hired. The next day, I skipped into work, knowing I had more than just a bigger wage packet to look forward to. The boy's name was Eric Whiting. As luck would have it, he lived just around the corner from the shop and at lunchtime, he invited me back to his place.

"You won't have time to go all the way back to yours," he added in explanation. "Boss wants us back for half one."

Beaming, I followed Eric to his parents' house, where we sat side by side and ate our packed lunches; mine was ham sandwiches with a bottle of lemonade. We chatted and laughed, and I got to like Eric more and more. It turned out he was just over a year older than me. One day, during our lunch hour, I helped him cut his jeans down into fringe shorts, ready for a trip to Scarborough with his mates.

"I'll send you a postcard," he promised with a wink.

Each morning, before work, I hovered by the front door, waiting for the postman, without really admitting to myself why. But when the postcard eventually came it had a saucy seaside slogan on the front, and my mother, Alma, hit the roof.

"I'm not having that filth on my mantlepiece," she said shortly. "It can go in the bin. The outside bin."

By now, I was 16, but still, for my age, painfully immature and naïve. I didn't even understand the joke on the postcard and was too embarrassed to ask Eric for an explanation. Each day, we continued to eat our lunches together, and though I liked Eric, I didn't expect anything more than friendship from him. I'd never had a boyfriend and didn't particularly want one either. Besides, I'd heard that Eric had a girlfriend already. I was happy with the way things were.

Some months later, I was allowed to go to the pub for the first time. For me, it was a big social occasion and there was a whole bunch of us there, including Eric and his girlfriend. When she saw me, taking my seat on a corner table, she marched over; hands on hips, lips pursed like a puffer fish.

"Well, you can have him!" she snarled.

And with that, whilst I was still trying to work out who or what she meant, she took a mouthful of her Coke and spat it out all over my white tights. I gasped, stunned, and ran to the toilets to rinse the stain out. The tights were nearly new, and I was panic-stricken, knowing Mam would kill me if they were ruined. It was only as I lathered up the hand soap that it slowly dawned on me; she had been talking about Eric. I felt a rush of delight and suddenly the tights did not matter at all. Though I was alone in the toilets, I allowed myself a little smile. My reflection grinned back at me from the mirror over the sink.

"You've got yourself a boyfriend, Joy," I whispered. "A boyfriend!"

* * *

From that evening onwards, Eric and I were inseparable. At weekends, we went on long bike rides, and we took his family's two Alsatian dogs out for walks. Eric was kind and funny, but responsible and reliable. Then, in the autumn of 1971, aged 17, I missed a period. And then another. I was overwhelmed too, with feelings of nausea and exhaustion. Secretly, on my way home from work, I made an appointment to see the doctor.

"You'll have to come with me," I said to Eric. "I think I'm having a baby."

His face blanched but he nodded and squeezed my hand.

"I'll be there," he promised.

The next day, when he met me outside the surgery, he was wearing a smart suit and tie. The sight of him was enough to defuse the tension, and I felt my worries floating away, like bubbles.

"I've never seen you wear a suit! I giggled. "It's only a doctor's appointment."

"First time for everything," Eric muttered nervously. "We need to make a good impression."

Unlike Eric, deep down, I had an unshakeable confidence that everything was going to be alright. When the doctor confirmed that I was indeed pregnant, I felt my face splitting into the biggest smile. I just couldn't help myself. The doctor tutted with some impatience and immediately offered me a termination.

"Absolutely not," I retorted, still beaming. "This is my baby and I'm keeping it."

There was no way I would have considered any other alternative. Even so, with every step of our walk home, the prospect of facing our parents loomed larger, and the bravado seeped out of me, drip by drip. By the time we reached Eric's house, I felt so scared, so alone. I was suddenly aware of how young we were.

"Let's tell your parents now," I whispered. "Get it over with."

He nodded, but I saw his jaw clench. He was almost as frightened as I was. Eric's mother, Ivy, was busy doing a crossword puzzle under a table lamp. His dad, Jim, was reading the newspaper. They were lovely people, and up to now had always welcomed me into their family, but I wasn't at all sure how they'd react to this bombshell.

"Go on," I hissed as Eric took a seat on the sofa. "Go on, say it!"

He sucked in his breath and said in a voice which tried, and miserably failed, to sound casual:

"Oh! Well, yeah! Joy is having a baby!"

There was a moment of terrifying silence and then Ivy threw her crossword book into the air and ran over to smother me with a hug.

"I said they were spending too much time together!" she laughed as Jim stood up to shake our hands. He huffed good-naturedly and said:

"Your brother's wife is pregnant. The cat's pregnant. And now Joy! What's going on?"

Buoyed by their enthusiasm, we went straight round to break the news to my own mother. My parents were separated, and Mam and I were very close. It was her reaction, and her blessing, that mattered to me above all others. I stood in the doorway, and simply burst into tears. I didn't say a word.

"You're pregnant," she said softly, and she took me in her arms. "Don't worry pet, it's going to be fine."

"We're getting married," Eric piped up, from behind me. "I won't let her down. I promise you that."

"You're far too young," Mam replied. "Don't be silly. You don't need to get married."

But she could see that Eric was serious and eventually, she came round to the idea, and she gave us her support. Deep down, I had always known that she would. She and I began planning my big day, and she took me to the market to choose a pink mini dress with a matching coat, which was the height of fashion. I ordered a single pink carnation too, and it went well with my long light brown hair. It was only a very small do, but our families were both invited and Eric's sister, Edith, was chosen as a witness. The wedding was booked for 9.10am on November 27 1971 at Middlesbrough register office. We couldn't afford wedding cars, or even a taxi, and the 272 bus into town was running late.

"Come on," I groaned, checking my watch as we stood, frozen in the bitter wind, at the bus stop. "Where's the bloody bus when you need it?"

I eventually arrived at the register office, breathless and flushed, with my nice outfit all rumpled.

"You're late," Eric smiled. "But you look gorgeous. You really do."

The following February, I turned 18. And that May, our first daughter, Donna, was born, at North Tees Hospital. She weighed 6lbs 4ozs and, as the midwife lifted her into the air, she looked as though she was clapping her tiny little hands together.

"Oh, you've got a clever one here," said the midwife.

I felt on top of the world. I couldn't wait to show my baby off, to push her down the street and bask in the warmth of the admiring glances that would come our way. I couldn't wait to dress her in the dainty doll-like clothes I'd been buying with my wages. Eric and I had been allocated a small council house, part of a tight-knit community on an estate in Stockton. The Friday nights were lively around there, especially after last orders in the pub, but the people were friendly, and I was looking forward to everyone on the street fussing over my baby. Once at home, of course, reality set in around me like concrete. I'd had no inkling of how hard it would be to raise a child, the sleepless nights, the colic, the nappy changes. I was on constant call. I loved my baby, I adored her, but I also felt as though I was drowning. I couldn't cope. One morning, at the end of my tether, I put Donna in the pram and walked the five-mile route to my mother's house.

"I'm exhausted, Mam," I told her tearfully. "I feel out of my depth."

"Here," she said, stretching out her arms. "Leave the baby with me. You go home and get some rest. You'll feel completely different after a decent night's sleep."

"You've no Moses basket or cot," I pointed out. "How will you manage?"

She pulled a big drawer out of her sideboard and emptied the contents onto the carpet.

"There," she smiled, popping a cushion into the drawer and laying Donna on the top. "Snug as a bug in a rug."

I envied her confidence and her easy way with Donna, but the more I tried to emulate it, the more anxious I seemed to become. It should have been a relief to have a night to myself. But instead, I felt lost, walking away from Mam's without my baby. I couldn't help thinking I had failed somehow, even though I knew that wasn't reasonable. And all night long, I worried that something might happen to Donna.

"She's perfectly safe," Eric reassured me. "Come back to bed, Joy."

Even after Donna came home, the following day, the alarm continued. I was plagued by vivid daydreams of the house setting on fire, or a burglar stealing my baby, or the pram tipping into the road as I walked to the shops. Each scenario was more irrational yet more convincing than the last. And as much as I found looking after my daughter exhausting, I couldn't bear to let her out of my sight and let other people help me. I was stuck, trapped in what felt like quicksand, without a hand to pull me out.

"I think you have a touch of postnatal depression," Mam frowned, when she visited next. "We should get the doctor."

The GP agreed with her, and I was prescribed medication, which, as the weeks passed, helped a little. I began to feel as though I could, at last, keep my head above the water. Eric and I were blissfully happy together too. We spent long evenings at home, in comfortable domesticity, him brushing my long fair hair whilst we watched TV. He got a job on the railways, clearing old sleepers, and he earned a decent wage. On Friday nights, to celebrate the start of the weekend, he'd bring me a box of my favourite Milk Tray chocolates.

"I'm a lucky girl," I told him, throwing my arms around him.

* * *

Early in 1973, I fell pregnant again and Eric and I were thrilled. By now, the depression had lifted completely, and I couldn't wait for a baby brother or sister for Donna. But 24 weeks in, I caught a bad case of German measles. I was feverish and weak, and I began losing weight at an alarming rate. There were no scans back then, but I was sent to hospital for urgent checks. A doctor leaned over me, with a stethoscope, to listen for the baby's heartbeat. And then, slowly and sadly, he shook his head. Time seemed to stand still, as though all the clocks had stopped, along with my baby's heart. I stared at him, wildly trying to find other reasons for his gloomy expression. But in my heart, I knew.

"I'm very sorry," he said.

I was booked in to give birth at the hospital the following day. On October 19, our baby boy was born sleeping. He was whisked away, and I did not even catch a glimpse of him. I never said hello. Or goodbye. All around me, on the ward, there were babies crying, and new mothers glowing with the first flush of motherhood. It struck me as so unspeakably cruel. My empty arms ached to hold my baby son. My bruised heart cried out for him.

'I will see you next year,' said a matter-of-fact midwife when Eric came to collect me.

"No way," I sobbed, as I packed my things. "I won't be having another baby. Not ever."

And yet over the next few months, the yearning grew. And grew. I longed for another child and Eric felt the same way too. In February 1974, I fell pregnant again. This time, I was nervous, ticking the days off on a calendar, hardly daring to hope I would make it full term. As the months passed, and my bump grew, I began to look forwards, at last.

One day in October, when I was almost at my due date, Donna, aged two, was peering out of the front window at home, standing on a stool, when she suddenly lost her balance and fell to the floor, banging her head. She screamed so loudly that I was sure she was seriously hurt. Startled and scared, I scooped her into my arms and dashed to Middlesbrough General Hospital.

"Don't worry," the doctor reassured me. "She's bruised, but fine. Looks like it's hit you worse than her."

He was right. The shock of seeing my precious daughter in a crumpled heap on the floor had been enough to trigger my labour, and before we left the A and E department, I felt the first twinges of contractions. I made a second dash, to a different hospital, where I was rushed into the maternity unit and midwives announced the baby was breech and needed to be turned. I was quickly sedated and taken to theatre for the procedure, which was luckily successful. Later that evening, my contractions grew closer and stronger until the pain felt like it was taking over my entire body and might just lift me clean off the bed.

"We're not making much progress," the midwife frowned.

She brought in a doctor who carried, what looked to me, like instruments of torture in his hands.

"We'd like to try a forceps delivery," he explained.

I shuddered but nodded. By now, I was so desperate, I was willing to try anything. Soon after, with what looked like large tongs easing her into the world, our second daughter, Jodey, was born.

It was October 16 – almost exactly a year since losing my baby son – and I thought back to the midwife's wise words as I was leaving the hospital.

'I will see you next year…'

She had been right, after all.

I reached out for a cuddle with my baby girl, but, as she was being examined by doctors, a hush fell in the delivery room.

"Her head and her eyes are very swollen," the midwife explained. "Hopefully she's just bruised from her rocky ride into the world. But it could be a cyst on the side of her head."

I was scared stiff. I hadn't anticipated anything like this. I had just presumed that if I could carry the baby full-term everything would be fine. Baby Jodey was whisked away before I could even hold her, and I was told she would need to spend the night in an intensive care unit, whilst the injury to her head was assessed.

Again, I had that awful and familiar empty feeling in my arms. I prayed, desperately, that this time, I would get to hold my baby. All night, I was wide awake, right through to first light, pleading with staff for news of her. I'd had a blood transfusion and wasn't well enough to be allowed out of bed and so not allowed to visit her myself. By the time the doctors did their morning round, they were able to give me the reassurance I'd been longing for.

"The swelling had subsided," they told me. "It's good news. It looks like it's not too serious after all. You should be able to see her later on today."

That first bonding cuddle with my new daughter was a moment of pure magic. Immediately, I was struck by the brilliance of her blue, blue, eyes. They sparkled at me, like genuine jewels. She stared at me, in wide-eyed wonderment, and I was sure she knew who I was. Whereas Donna looked just like her daddy, Jodey looked a little more like me.

"You're beautiful," I whispered.

I felt so lucky, so blessed. Holding Jodey tenderly in my arms, I vowed to love her and to protect her with every breath in my body.

"Nobody will ever hurt you," I promised. "Nobody will ever make you cry. Not whilst I'm around."

\* \* \*

After we got home, Jodey's bruising fortunately cleared up completely. I adjusted to life as a busy mother of two and I quickly realised the differences between my two daughters ran further than skin-deep. Even as a baby, Jodey was completely opposite in character to Donna. Jodey was wilful and determined and would grizzle and scream in her cot until she got some attention. Donna, placid and accepting, simply went with the flow.

"If I'd had Jodey first, she'd have been an only child," I used to joke.

Thankfully, though the worry had lurked at the back of my mind during the entire pregnancy, I had no postnatal depression this time. But even so, Jodey kept me on my toes. If I put her in the cot, she would yell and screech until I picked her up again for a cuddle. Many nights, I was up for maybe two or three hours whilst the world slept, singing softly to Jodey and rocking her in my arms. She was perfectly content as long as she was being snuggled. It was only after I laid her back in the cot, that her blue eyes would snap wide open, and the wailing would begin again. It was as if she needed that human warmth, that constant contact, to give her reassurance.

"Do you think she's OK?" I asked Mam anxiously. "She's very demanding."

"All babies are different," she replied. "Donna was such a good baby, so Jodey is bound to seem more hands-on. That's all it is, love."

And when Jodey began crawling, and then toddling around, she was a real handful. I had to follow her everywhere as if we were surgically attached.

"You need eyes in the back of your head with Jodey-Podey," Mam laughed.

That was our nickname for her and often I would sing her name out rather than say it. One morning, I found her snagged, by her nappy, on the outside of her cot. She had obviously tried to escape, a moment earlier, and been caught on her way down.

"Jodey!" I squealed. "You could have hurt yourself!"

Another time, before dawn, she climbed out of her cot and toddled her way downstairs to try to put some music on the radio. Of course she couldn't reach the radio, and I wasn't far behind her on the stairs. I felt as though I slept with one eye open and one ear always listening; as soon as I heard the slightest noise, I knew that Jodey was up to mischief. She loved music, and whilst I was clearing up after breakfast, she would dance in her pyjamas to Elton John and Abba. Donna, serious and quiet, would sit on the sofa with her toast, and watch.

"I'm glad I can keep an eye on one of you, at least," I told Donna.

One day, soon after Jodey's third birthday, I was busy cleaning downstairs and I realised she had gone suspiciously quiet. I found her in my bedroom, her cute face painted in technicolour with my make-up; lipsticks ground into the carpet, eyeshadows scattered across the bedspread.

"You're a little terror!" I told her.

She was always up to something. She was fascinated by animals, especially dogs, and when we went out, she insisted on stroking every single pet she saw. Sometimes it could take me an hour just to get to the corner shop and back, because Jodey would stop and make a fuss of all the dogs we met along the way. And of course, inevitably, on one walk, a dog nipped at her hand and made her cry. It wasn't serious, but I hoped she might learn her lesson, and not approach strange dogs with such enthusiasm in the future.

But the next time we went out, she ran over and hugged the very first dog she saw, as if to let him know there were no hard feelings! I shook my head and said:

"I don't know what I'm going to do with you, Jodey-Podey."

At Mam's house, Jodey tripped up one day whilst she was carrying a pencil, and it pierced the side of her cheek. There was a little hole in the flesh which sent waves of alarm through me. My heart racing, tears streaming down my face, I arrived at A&E, carrying her in my arms. I considered myself responsible. She seemed to have one mishap after another. It seemed as though I spent my entire life keeping her under surveillance and yet she kept on getting into bother.

"Some kids are just accident prone," said a smiling nurse. "She's fine. Her cheek will heal in a day or two."

Another time, I found Jodey in the kitchen, teetering on a dining chair, with a half-empty bottle of cough medicine in her chubby little hand. Her mouth was pink and sticky, and she was laughing at her own misdemeanour.

"Jodey!" I screeched.

I had taken my eyes off her for only two minutes, just to put some washing in, yet she had managed to drag a chair along to the high medicine cupboard and swallow a few mouthfuls of the liquid. In horror, I called for an ambulance. As we waited, I chastised myself. I was so angry that I'd let it happen. I could only hope that she would be OK.

"Children's cough medicine is usually harmless," said the paramedic who arrived to check Jodey over. "Keep an eye on her but I really don't think there is any serious harm done."

It appeared to be another let-off, another near miss.

"I'm going to glue you down," I said, waggling my finger at Jodey. "I can't cope with all these dramas."

# 2
# Sensitive Soul

By the time Donna started school, aged four, she could read, and she soon became an avid little bookworm. We had a large cupboard in the living room and Donna would hide herself away in there, with a book, a torch and a chocolate biscuit. She could entertain herself quite contentedly for hours. She was so quiet and well-behaved that often I had to check on her with my own torch, just for my own peace of mind. Jodey, meanwhile, was like a whirlwind around the house, usually up to no good, and always trying to rope Donna in, to go along with her pranks.

One of her favourite tricks was to lean into the cupboard to ask her big sister a question, and when poor Donna opened her mouth, Jodey would squirt in some ketchup or maybe some salad dressing. Her jokes were always light-hearted and well-meaning; her pranks were slapstick rather than cruel and calculating. But even so, she was always in some sort of trouble. I'd hear Donna screaming in protest from inside her reading cupboard and it was a sure sign that Jodey was tormenting her once again.

"I'm just playing," Jodey always insisted.

She didn't understand that not everyone shared the same outlook as her. Even before she started school, Jodey showed a true affection for babies and animals. She had a row of dolls in her bedroom which she adored. She bathed, dressed and fed them, cuddled them, sang to them and told them stories, as though they were real babies. And yet, she was little more than a baby herself.

"You'll make a wonderful Mammy one day, Jodey-Podey," I told her.

We had a beautiful Alsatian dog, named Zorba, a gift from Eric's family. Zorba would be made to sit patiently whilst Jodey buttoned him up in little dresses and cardigans. She even made him wear a hat and a scarf in the winter.

"It's a good job that dog is so easy-going," I laughed.

Sometimes, Jodey would even enlist Donna to help her lift the animal into her old baby pram, and strap him in. He looked so comical, with his paws poking out from under the rain-cover, and a look of good-natured resignation in his big liquid eyes. She was hardly big enough to reach the pram handle, but she would proudly wheel him up and down our street so that the neighbours could stop and exclaim what a lovely baby he was, albeit a little hairy.

"Good doggy!" she shouted. "Go to sleep!"

By now, we had moved to a bigger house, a three-bedroomed semi, on another council estate, but the area was run-down and severely deprived. There was rising unemployment too and many families around us were crippled by poverty and social hardship. Nationally, there were growing calls for strikes and protests, and, everywhere, there was a general feeling of despair. On our estate, there was an empty house, which had been vacated in a hurry, for some reason. There was an abandoned vegetable patch at the back of the house and together with our neighbours, we dug up potatoes and swedes. It was free food, though basic, and nobody could afford to turn it down. Most people didn't have the luxury of pride, and of picking and choosing where their meals came from.

There was a fuel shortage too, and even when the coalman made an appearance on the street, we often couldn't afford his spiralling prices. One evening, Eric brought home railway sleepers from a rubbish pile at work, and he chopped them up for firewood and shared them around the neighbourhood. Again, nobody was too proud to refuse. It was a miserable time for our region, and beyond, and yet we were far luckier than many on our estate. We had one reliable wage coming in, and we had support from our families too.

The Winter of Discontent arrived in 1978, with widespread strikes and freezing temperatures combining to form a gloomy smog over the whole of the North-East. The daily news was depressingly predictable. And yet for me, in my own little bubble, this was such a happy time. I had two beautiful daughters and a loving husband, and just about enough money to get by. This was all I had ever wanted; my own little family. I pinched myself, each night, to remind myself how lucky I was.

But then, just as the country seemed to be rallying, economically and socially, my own life, conversely, began to disintegrate. It was as though I was on a completely different trajectory to everyone else. I fell pregnant again but, before we could get used to the news, I suffered an early miscarriage, and it was very distressing. And though Mam was supportive and sympathetic, Eric seemed quite distant and we began to bicker and argue in a way we never had before. Like a lot of men, he struggled to understand that for me, a miscarriage, no matter how early, was the loss of a child. I mourned not so much for what I had lost, but for what I would never have, for the life that would never be. The miscarriage also brought back raw memories of our still-born son, and I grieved for him and missed him, all over again.

"You just don't get it, do you?" I said to Eric.

Until now, we had been a tight family unit, always on the same side. Now, I was not so sure. In the supermarkets, prices went up sharply, and it was a strain to make ends meet. Each week, Eric would give me half of his wages as housekeeping. He kept the other half for himself.

"I can't do the shopping and pay the rent and cover everything else," I complained. "Prices have gone up. Wages haven't. There just isn't enough to go around. Not anymore."

Now, in today's society, it would be almost unthinkable for a man to keep back half of his wages and such behaviour would no doubt be viewed as selfish and sexist. But in the context of that time, in the late 70s, it was perfectly accept-able. Eric was a good man and a loving father, and he was only behaving in exactly the same way as his friends and his family did. Most men kept half their wages; it was accepted and more than that, it was expected of them. And so, most women had to perform minor domestic miracles to make the housekeeping allocation last from week to week. I knew my house was no different to any other. Even so, the resentment crept in, uninvited, like mould. We needed school shoes for Donna and a winter coat for Jodey. The boiler was on the blink, and the bathroom window didn't shut properly. The list was endless, and my own minor needs didn't seem to figure on it anywhere. To add insult to injury, I was working part-time myself too. Mam would babysit, free of charge, whilst I did shifts in a packaging factory. It just didn't seem fair and I was becoming more and more unhappy.

"That's how it is," Mam told me, with a weary shake of her head.

Though she thought it unjust, she was accepting, and there was no thought in her mind that it would or could change. One week, I didn't have enough money to pay the rent, and I'd just about had enough of scrimping and saving. Without telling Eric, I carried it over to the next week, hoping for a short-term windfall from God knows where. I even marked the rent as 'paid' in the rent book, mimicking the usual stamp, to ease my guilt. And as the days passed, and I thought of the rent book, hidden away underneath my sewing tin, a place Eric would never look, I almost convinced myself that I had paid it. After that first nerve-shredding gamble, it became easier and easier to tell myself that everything was OK. Perhaps I would never be found out. Perhaps I could hoodwink the rent man, as easily as I had hoodwinked Eric, and indeed myself. Perhaps the world would end, and none of this would matter. I placated myself with whatever excuse I could pluck most easily out of the ether. But one day, I came home from the school-run to find Eric waving the rent book angrily in the air.

"What on earth is going on, Joy?" he asked.

My stomach plunged. He'd had a call from the landlord and my deception was unravelling right before my eyes like a ball of wool.

"I couldn't afford it," I explained hastily. "I just pretended it was paid. Silly, I know. I didn't know what else to do."

We had a huge row, Eric blaming me, me blaming him, and that night, as he snored beside me, the worries swirled around my mind, and I didn't sleep at all. Staring at a large crack, running the length of our ceiling, I wondered how on earth I was going to get out of this mess. That crack seemed to sum everything up perfectly; my cosy dream of married bliss was fracturing around me. The following morning, by 7am, I had strapped Jodey into the pram, with Donna sitting on the top, her favourite book on her lap. By now, we lived around six miles from Mam, but I walked all the way, my resolve strengthening with every step.

"I've left Eric," I announced when she came to the door. "And I'm not going back. No way."

"Come inside," she sighed. "Have a brew. Let's talk it through."

She knew better than to try to talk me out of it straight-away. And Eric knew me well enough to know exactly where to find me. He came straight to Mam's after he had finished his shift.

"You're my wife and I want you to come home please," he said, with a tone that said he would not back down.

At first, I stood firm. A petty part of me thought he was only here because he was hungry, and he wanted me to cook his tea. But as he spoke, and I saw his blue eyes misting with emotion, I felt myself softening.

"Please Joy," he said. "Please come back."

I relented and we walked home together; Donna on his shoulders, Jodey straining to get out of the pram and toddle alongside us. The rent fiasco meant that we had to move house yet again, this time to a privately rented flat. The neighbours soon made it clear that the block wasn't child-friendly, especially towards a little girl like Jodey who liked to run up and down the balcony, shouting loudly at everyone she met. Months later, we were on the move again. There had been a distance between Eric and I since that first short split, and our relationship was up and down. We argued about money mostly. But we were moving in opposing directions too; we had married so young, with our characters as yet unformed, and now we were maturing differently. We seemed to fall out more and more and, eventually, we decided to separate. I found myself once again at Mam's door, but after a few weeks cramped up and sleeping in her living room with the girls, I accepted a place in a hostel.

"Are you sure, Joy?" Mam asked anxiously. "You know you're welcome to stay here."

I nodded gratefully, but I knew that there wasn't enough room at her house. And part of me wanted to be a bit more independent, to show everyone that I could cope on my own. If this was my future, as a single mother, it was best to embrace it.

"Oh, you know me, I'll be alright," I promised her, with an assurance I didn't really feel.

\* \* \*

Yet it turned out, as is often the case, that the idea of the hostel was much worse than the reality. We were allocated our own room with bunk beds and a single bed, and though it was basic it was clean. There was a nursery room, where all the little ones could play together. Jodey, of course, loved throwing herself into the rough and tumble, whilst Donna, always more solitary, preferred to read on her bunk bed. The hostel was for mothers and children only, and we were all handed our own chores to keep the place running smoothly. It was my job to mop the stairs and the passage-ways. In some ways, there was a strong sense of belonging and community; we were all women going through a bad time, worrying about our kids, fretting about where the next meal would come from. Sure, there were trouble-makers and idiots in there, just like in all walks of life, but most of the women, like me, were just trying to make the best of a difficult situation. There was a camaraderie in chatting at night over a brew, comparing and condemning the men in our lives.

I had at least two jobs on the go during that time; in various shops and bars, and I did some cleaning work too. Mam, as always, was on hand to babysit.

"I don't know where I would be without you," I told her.

And I had lots of support from Eric too, he never let his children down. Despite the problems between us he saw them every weekend and made sure he took them out perhaps to the cinema or to the park. It was on one Sunday night, as he was handing the children over outside the hostel, that he said:

"This is silly, Joy. Why don't you have a think about coming back to me? Trying again? I hate the thought of you in here."

I felt a warm flush of delight, which travelled right up from my toes and into my cheeks. I had been thinking the exact same thing for weeks. It was the summer of 1977 when we got another new place, this time on another estate. Our move went well, the children settled in quickly, and our new place felt like a second chance.

"Let's try for a baby," I said to Eric. "A fresh start for us both."

As long as it's a boy this time," he joked.

Some weeks later, I had a routine smear test and was alarmed to be called back to see the doctor in person for the results.

"We've found pre-cancerous cells," explained the GP. "No need to panic just yet, but we do need to keep a close eye on you. Watch and wait."

It was an anxious bus ride home. I was only 23 years old and facing cervical cancer. Despite the doctor's assurances that it was in the early stages, I was petrified. Most of all, the fear of leaving my two little girls without a mother lay heavy on me.

"We'll have to put off our plans for another baby," Eric said, when I got home. "Your health is more important."

I nodded numbly. But the very next month, my period was late. And I could already feel the tell-tale backache and nausea that came with early pregnancy. I realised I must have been pregnant before I'd even got the results of the smear test.

"Are you sure you want to go ahead with this baby?" asked my doctor.

I nodded firmly.

"Absolutely," I said. "This is a new life."

Even so, it was a worrying time. I couldn't enjoy the pregnancy at all. As I watched my bump grow, I envisaged a tumour growing at the same rate inside me, and it sent a ripple of panic through me.

"Hang in there," I whispered to the baby. "Mammy will look after you."

It was decided that I would give birth by caesarean section and undergo a complete hysterectomy at the same time. It was nerve-wracking but I was also relieved to be getting rid of the threat of cancer, once and for all. Our son, Jamie, was born on March 31, 1978. I had worried he might have been affected in some way by my illness, but he was perfectly healthy, and beautiful too, just like his sisters. Eric, who had waited at home whilst I had surgery, went out to celebrate the birth with his mates.

"A boy at last!" he yelled, when I phoned him with the news. "Are you sure? Have you checked and double-checked inside that nappy?"

Much as he adored his two girls, he was euphoric to have a son, and at first, Jamie's birth brought Eric and I closer together. But as I recovered from the hysterecto-my, I lost lots of weight. I was a petite build to start with, usually weighing only around eight stones, but I quickly dropped down to six, and I became far too thin. I felt very anxious again, just as I had after Donna was born, and I grew obsessed with handwashing and cleaning. I spent so much time with my hands submerged in water that they became red raw. I had to turn plugs and light switches on and off, on and off. It was wearying, but I became convinced that if I didn't follow the routine, something terrible would happen to one of the children. Eric was worried about me, and he didn't know what to do for the best.

"You're driving me mad with this," he sighed.

"I'm driving myself mad," I replied. "But I don't know how to stop it."

* * *

The months passed and slowly my health returned almost to normal, though I still suffered with random and irrational bursts of fear. I tried hard to concentrate on raising my three children, and the role brought me more happiness and fulfilment than I could ever have dreamed. For me, being a mother was all I had ever wanted in life. The girls loved having a baby brother and Jodey in particular fussed over Jamie constantly. Though she was only four years old herself when he was born, the maternal instinct shone out of her. She would sit on the sofa and slap her fat little knees expectantly; that was her sign for me to lay Jamie across her legs for a cuddle. And the moment I took him back from her, she would smack her knees again and shout:

"More baby! More!"

She was incredibly affectionate and protective towards him, and when she started school, her biggest concern was not her own new environment, but rather leaving Jamie behind at home all day. It didn't help that she wasn't keen on school at all. She struggled to sit still in class, and she didn't enjoy learning to read and write one bit. She and Donna were chalk and cheese; the gap between their personalities widening with each year, and yet the bond they shared remained strong.

In those early years, we were much like every other family. Every time the children had a birthday, I made a cake and we invited friends for a little party. For Jodey's sixth birthday, Mam bought her a life-like baby doll, and

Jodey immediately christened her Tracey. Baby Tracey came out in the pram, alongside Jamie in his, every time we went to the shops. Jodey took great care in wrapping her up in cold weather, making sure she had a changing bag and a spare nappy in case of emergencies. And she would glare daggers at anyone with a loud voice who woke up Tracey by mistake.

"She's my baby," she explained, in a hushed voice. "She's sleeping. Be quiet please."

Even when she was in infant school, the two opposing sides of Jodey's character were already clear to see. She had boundless patience and tenderness with babies, dolls and animals, and indeed showed a maturity way beyond her years when she was looking after Jamie at home. And yet, in school, she found it impossible to sit quietly and pay attention. She was forever in trouble for not listening. At home, she would throw dramatic tantrums, seemingly with little or no provocation. She showed flashes of anger that came and faded just as quickly and inexplicably as they had arrived. Jodey had never really grown out of that baby stage where she would whine and wail in the cot until somebody picked her up for a cuddle. There was a sharp and jarring dichotomy between the two aspects of her personality, which I could only hope would ease as she grew older.

The following summer, in 1981, Eric got some cheap ferry tickets as a perk of his job on the railways. We had friends who had moved to Holland, again through Eric's job, and so we decided to make a holiday out of visiting them. We'd never been abroad before with the children, and I thought they would be thrilled at the prospect. But when I announced the news, Jodey looked at me as though I had lost control of my senses.

"I'm not going on a boat!" she protested. "No way! What about the sharks?"

We'd recently – and unwisely – let her watch the film *Jaws* and it had frightened her so much that she'd crept into bed with us for the next few nights. Now, I was realising it had left a lasting impression on her.

"That was just a film," I reminded her. "It's a plastic fish, Jodey!"

I felt sure she would calm down, with the promise of an adventure abroad, but if anything, as the date drew nearer, she just got worse. Her resistance seemed to be completely out of proportion. Each time I mentioned the holiday, she would throw screaming fits, lying on the floor, crying and yelling, until I was genuinely convinced she would make herself ill.

"I want to stay with Nanna," she pleaded. "Don't make me go. Please."

I didn't know what to do for the best. For a while, I tried to stay firm with her, to insist she came with us. But I could see she was never going to accept it. At the last minute, I relented, and Jodey stayed behind with her grandmother.

"She's such a sensitive soul," Mam said to me. "We need to be careful with her."

She, too, felt there was something a little different about Jodey, something which made her more delicate, more vulnerable, than other children. But it was hard to put it into words exactly.

Jamie had by now started nursery school himself, and he came home one day complaining that he was being picked on by some bigger kids.

"Don't take any notice," I told him. "They're not worth it."

But the next morning, I got a call from school to say that Jodey had marched into Jamie's classroom, yanked the bullies out of their chairs and given them a blistering piece of her mind.

"I'm sorry," I said to the teacher. "She does the wrong things for the right reasons. It won't happen again, I promise."

Jamie came home from school that night glowing with pride, and the sort of satisfaction that comes from having an older sister on your side.

"They won't be bothering you again," Jodey said triumphantly.

It was yet another example of a curious mix of character; she was a big softie in many ways, but with a streak of granite running through her. She couldn't bear to see people she loved treated badly, and that included her siblings, her dolls and her pets. She would always step in and stand up for them. Yet for all her superficial bravado, for all her confidence, she had a unique fragility. Scratch beneath the surface, sweep aside the bluster, and she was very unsure of herself. I could see her vulnerability, and it pulled at my heart. I could only hope, as she got older, that she would stand up for herself in the same way she had for her brother.

* * *

For Jodey's seventh birthday, in October 1981, I baked her a Magic Roundabout cake, and she got another new doll. Before going to bed each night, she kissed each of her dolls religiously and sometimes, I would hover outside her bedroom door to listen to her talking softly as she tucked them in. She had such a gentle and tender nature.

"If you need me in the night, just shout for Mammy," she told them.

It made me smile. She was repeating to her dolls the exact same phrases which I used with her. But in school, her teachers were complaining, more and more, that she was disruptive and naughty. She wasn't making much progress academically, which they didn't understand, since Donna was doing so well.

"Jodey has such a short concentration span," they said. "She can't even stay still and listen to a story. If she's on a chair, she's fidgeting and distracting other children. Most of the time, she won't even sit down."

I had noticed the same problems at home.

"She'll grow out of it," I told myself. "She's only small yet."

By the time Jodey was nine years old, Eric and I had decided to split for good. Our relationship had been slowly crumbling, right since that first row over the rent book. We had limped on, and tried and tried again, for the sake of the kids. But this time, we both knew it was over. Eric moved into a place nearby and he saw the kids at least every weekend and sometimes more often. He took them out, he booked treats and holidays and though our relationship had failed, I couldn't fault him as a father.

"Can we stay friends?" he asked, and I nodded readily.

It was what we both wanted. The children and I moved again, this time into a nice modern three-bedroom house. Jodey was still not a big fan of school, and I dreaded the calls and notes from her teachers. But she loved playing out, and most afternoons she was out in the street with a big group of pals; she was as sociable as Donna was shy. One afternoon, she puffed through the back door, dragging a black bin bag behind her.

"Look Mam!" she announced. "A whole bag of baby clothes for my dollies!"

I stared suspiciously as she began unpacking lovely little dresses with matching cardigans and socks.

"Where did you get all those?" I asked.

"They were left out on the street for the binmen," she said. "Good job I found them. My Tracey will love this dress."

She was already holding outfits up against her dollies, checking for size and suitability.

"Well, we'd better put them all through the wash," I said. "Goodness knows who left those out for the bin. They look good as new."

Just then, there was a knock at the front door, and I found a lady waiting on the path.

"I think you have a bag of my baby clothes," she said hesitantly. "Only we're in the middle of moving house, and we left it out on the pavement for a few minutes. I was told your little girl might have them?"

I flushed with embarrassment.

"I am so sorry," I babbled. "Really, I can't believe it. Jodey told me they were left out as rubbish."

Hurriedly, I packed the clothes and handed them back, and I made Jodey issue a half-hearted apology at the door too.

"My dollies would have loved those clothes," she said wistfully.

"It's an important lesson," I said, trying not to laugh despite myself. "Don't take what doesn't belong to you. You should have checked first."

Even aged 11, as she approached the end of her time at primary school, Jodey still loved playing with her dolls above anything else. She didn't care that many of her friends by now thought it was babyish and embarrassing. We had a new puppy too, an Alsatian-Collie named Rex. Jodey had an old orange and black tartan pram and she often managed to squash Rex into the pram, alongside her many dollies. The poor dog was resigned to it; he never objected, even when she popped four socks on his paws.

"You behave, now," she told him sternly, as she wheeled him out of the front door and into the sunshine. "Any messing and there's no treats."

# 3
# Temper Tantrums

In September 1986, Jodey followed Donna on to Albany Secondary Modern, in Norton, Stockton-on-Tees. High school is a big step for any child, and I hoped she might show signs of growing up a little. Donna, certainly, had matured and made good progress after moving schools. Jodey had an October birthday too, she was one of the oldest in her year, and so I hoped the change might come quickly.

"Time to be a big girl now," I told her, as I straightened her tie, ready for her first day.

But even as I said it, the words sounded unconvincing. And if anything, even within that first year, the reverse started to happen with Jodey. Her temper had always been fiery, and I was used to her throwing dramatic tantrums when things didn't go her way. At the back of my mind, I had always told myself, or maybe I had kidded myself, that she would grow out of them, as most children do, by the time she got to high school. But now, her behaviour seemed to get worse, and I was becoming concerned about her. Her teachers didn't seem to think she was learning much at all. Though she was pleasant and happy, and she had lots of friends, they had the same complaints as her primary school teachers; she didn't listen, she couldn't concentrate, her work was of a poor standard. She was lagging behind academically and emotionally. The list went on and on.

"I know," I told them wearily. "I'm doing my best, really I am."

Jodey's reports were as bad as Donna's were good. I was conscious that she wasn't made to feel the pressure of Donna's achievements, and that she wasn't under her big sister's shadow, academically. But that didn't really seem to be the case. Jodey was very much her own person. It was an odd thing to say, but she was quite content the way she was, tantrums and all.

"Jodey has her own way of doing things," I told her teachers, again and again. I was aware I sounded like a stuck record. "I'm sure she'll grow out of it. Eventually."

The slightest little thing could set her off too. Her favourite snack was a pikelet, a type of crumpet, with cheese melted on the top. One Saturday morning, she flipped open the bread bin and immediately began wailing when she couldn't find any crumpets.

"I'll go shopping later," I promised her.

But she was inconsolable. She lay down right there on the kitchen floor with her hands over her face and cried and cried.

"Jodey, it's not the end of the world," I said impatiently. "You need to stop throwing these hissy fits. You're a big girl now."

I went off to work, and, when I came home with the pikelets, she was still lying on the floor.

"For goodness' sake, Jodey!" I exclaimed. "Get up! Look, I'm grating the cheese for you now. It won't take long."

She gave me a tear-stained smile, but I didn't smile back. I wanted to try to shame her into better behaviour. But deep down, I was forming the opinion that this was about more than simply bad behaviour. I was starting to worry that there was something more serious wrong with my daughter. The next day, I called in to see Eric and confided in him.

"She ought to be over these tantrums," I said to him. "It's like she's stuck in the terrible twos. She's 13 years old for goodness sake!"

"I know," Eric nodded.

Like me, he was convinced there was a missing piece to this jigsaw; something that we didn't yet know. But all I could do, in the meantime, was manage Jodey's meltdowns the best I could.

Then one morning, she screamed herself hoarse because the video recorder had glitched and had failed to record her weekly favourite: *Top Of The Pops*.

"That's it!" she yelled dramatically, throwing herself onto the couch so forcefully I thought she might bounce right back.

This time, she cried and sobbed so much that she began coughing up blood. It was only a small amount, probably caused by her throat becoming hoarse and sore. But I was certain now that this was symptomatic of something far more serious, and I called the doctors and made an appointment. Hours later, Jodey was still wailing, all the way to the surgery, and even when we sat down in the waiting room. I was starting to feel desperate. What on earth was wrong with her?

"Please Jodey," I hissed. "Stop this awful noise. Please."

The receptionist shot me a disapproving glare and all at once I shrank back in my plastic chair. It appeared as though all eyes were on me, as though I was being judged; a single mother who couldn't control her kids. I wanted to stand on my chair and shout and tell them just how much I loved her and just how hard I was trying. But of course that would have been playing right into their hands and confirming their worst impressions of me.

"Jodey," I pleaded again. You're making yourself ill. Nobody wants to listen to this racket!"

But it made no difference. By now, we were entertainment for the entire waiting room and my cheeks were burning with shame. Jamie sat next to me, running his toy car over the seats, completely oblivious to the noise. I felt even more inadequate as a mother. He was so used to this chaos that he didn't even find it unusual.

"Jodey Whiting!" called the receptionist with a frown.

It was such a relief when our turn came but, inside the consultation room, I struggled to make myself heard over Jodey's screams. The doctor was middle-aged, with a ruddy face and wobbly jowls, and he looked extremely grumpy. He fixed me with a cold, self-righteous stare and, again, I felt like a complete failure.

"I'm worried about her..." I began, but my voice was drowned out.

The doctor waved me aside, leaned over to Jodey, who was lying on the floor, and, whipping off his shoe, suddenly shouted:

"I will make her shut up!"

He waved his shoe menacingly in her direction and little Jamie, who was clutching at my hand, let out a squeak of terror like a frightened fieldmouse. But Jodey, apart from perhaps a momentary pause for breath, carried on screeching. The doctor chased us out of his surgery with a lopsided run, one shoe on and shoe off. Jodey was screaming just as loudly as we left as when we had arrived. The only difference now was that Jamie was bawling too. My last memory, as we flew through the main doors, was of the receptionist shaking her head at me in disgust. It is only looking back that I can see the comedy in that scene. Back then, I felt wretched; I was at the end of my tether with nobody to turn to. I felt sure that my daughter was not simply a naughty child. I knew she had problems, and she needed support, not discipline. Yet I couldn't find anyone to listen. And certainly a shoe-waving doctor was not the answer.

\* \* \*

In the spring of 1987, my beloved mother became very sick. She had been diagnosed three years earlier with cancer and had at first been given only six months to live. She had fought on, gratefully accepting every treatment offered, and somehow the months stretched into years. During the last few weeks of her life I stayed with her every night. On one occasion, Jodey had been looking after her, whilst I was at work, and Mam had collapsed. Even though she was only 12, Jodey had phoned an ambulance, made her Nanna comfortable, and then brought a neighbour to help. Mam had rallied after a day or two in hospital, and she was filled with praise for Jodey.

"Honestly, I couldn't have had better care from a qualified doctor," she insisted. "That girl is a gemstone."

It was another example of the two extremes of Jodey. One day, she could be bawling her head off in public, the next, she was showing empathy and maturity beyond her years.

Sadly, Mam passed away in April 1987, aged only 62. We all missed her terribly. She had been a big part of the children's lives and a wonderful mother and grandmother.

A couple of months on, we moved again to another three-bedroom house, this time on the Tilery Estate, which would, many years later, become notorious as the setting for the TV show *Benefits Street*. I could not have begun to imagine the cruel irony this would later turn out to be for Jodey. That October, she became a teenager, and I was bowled over by the stunning young woman she was blossoming into. We dropped her childhood nickname of 'Jodey-Podey' and instead shortened it simply to 'Jode.' It felt more grown up. Her long brown hair was wavy, like mine, and her eyes were an arresting sapphire blue. Now that she was 13, I hoped that we might be able to iron out her behaviour problems once and for all. And there were some promising signs. In many ways, Jodey was incredibly grown-up and sensible. By now, she was being roped in to babysit for neighbouring families, and they all agreed Jodey was the best sitter they'd ever had.

"Honestly, she's first choice with me, and with my kids," my neighbour told me.

Not only was Jodey fun and caring, but she was trustworthy and reliable too. The children on the estate all loved her and it seemed to me she always had a little one either toddling along beside her or in a pushchair. At a moment's notice, if someone had a drama and needed a baby-sitter,

Jodey was there. She didn't even do it for the money. She did it for love, she did it simply because it was a part of who she was. On Saturday mornings, when many of her pals were lying in bed, Jodey would be out on the park with the little ones, pushing the swings, or lining them up for endless games of tag and football. Everyone knew her.

"Honestly, we'd trust Jodey with our children's lives," said another neighbour. "She's a treasure."

And yet, the contradictions were still there. She would lose her temper and throw herself on the carpet if she didn't get her own way. Though she was popular at school, and the teachers liked her, she was often in trouble for being chatty or distracted.

"She spends too long chatting with her pals and not long enough reading her textbooks," one teacher told me.

I clucked sympathetically, but I couldn't really see what else I could do.

"She's a good girl really," I protested. "She can't help herself."

I could see that nobody else believed me. Sometimes, it felt like me and Jodey against the world. Like her, I was torn between two opposing and conflicting schools of thought. Part of me wanted so much to believe that she was simply a challenging girl who would grow out of her problems in her own time. Another, more insistent part of me, felt that Jodey had a very real and physical trigger for her issues, and that they were, for the most part, beyond her control.

It was around this time that I began suffering with increased anxiety, which mutated, quickly, into full-blown panic attacks. My friends suggested that they were triggered by all the stress over Jodey, but really, I felt the problem had been lying dormant ever since the postnatal depression I'd suffered as a first-time parent with Donna. At first, I tried to block it out. The OCD tendencies re-emerged, stronger than ever, and they seemed to control everything I did. I battled against them, silently, defiantly, believing that acknowledging them would be in some way giving in to them. But as the days passed, I felt as though I was being pulled under by a riptide, and the more I struggled, the worse it got. Each night, after I'd gone to bed, I had to tiptoe back downstairs, five, six, seven times, to flick the light switches and plugs, again and again and again. I spent most of the night painfully wide awake, worrying, and the next day I was too weary and drained to even think about addressing the problem. Leaving the house each morning was a drawn-out fiasco and a punishing routine. I was forever locking and unlocking the door, then running back into the kitchen to check the plugs were off and the place was safe. Jamie was late for school, and I was late for work several times, because I just couldn't trust myself to lock the front door and walk away.

"What am I going to do?" I fretted.

Surprisingly, or perhaps not, it was Jodey who noticed how much I was struggling.

"You need to go to the doctor, Mam," she said. "Make an appointment and I'll come with you. We'll do it together."

At first, I wasn't sure about confiding in a doctor. I was embarrassed at what they might think of me. But Jodey reassured me, and she insisted on it. I had moved to a new surgery after the shoe-waving incident and, this time, I need not have worried. My GP was compassionate and kind and arranged for me to have a course of treatment, as an in-patient. Eric offered to have the children and Jodey, true to her word, came with me to see the doctor and afterwards, when I spent six weeks in hospital, she came to visit me every day after school.

"We'll soon have you home, Mam," she smiled.

This side of her just did not marry at all with the girl who screamed and yelled and rolled on the floor over something as trivial as missing out on the last chocolate biscuit. She had such a confusing contrast of emotions swirling around inside her and whilst it was difficult for the people around her, I knew it must be far more so for her. One moment, she was the responsible babysitter. The next, she was behaving like one of her toddler charges. Her behaviour went from one extreme to another; from serene to screaming, from loving to livid, and all in the click of a finger.

It was completely baffling to me. And no doubt to her too.

\* \* \*

It wasn't long after her 13th birthday that I noticed that Jodey was holding her right shoulder slightly higher than the other, and she was stooping a little too when she walked. She had never been a particularly well-co-ordinated child, but I had put that down to nature. I was always mindful, too, of the swelling on her head when she was born. I felt, instinctively, that the trauma of her birth might well have an impact on her as she grew up. At first though, I thought that the problem with her shoulder could be a consequence of puberty; Jodey was changing shape, growing into a young woman, and was possibly bashful or shy about her new shaped figure.

"Are you holding your shoulder down on purpose?" I asked her.

She shook her head, but I wasn't so sure. Yet as the weeks went on, I began to doubt myself. The drop in her shoulder became more pronounced, and next she started complaining of a pain in her back.

"It's keeping me awake at night," she said.

We saw our GP who said initially that he would monitor the situation, and then, after our next appointment, she was referred to see a specialist. Jodey was eventually diagnosed, just before she turned 14, with scoliosis, a curvature of the spine.

"We don't need to do much at this stage," said her consultant. "She may well need a rod in her back when she's finished growing. Let's keep an eye on her."

After the diagnosis, Jodey had regular appointments at the hospital. It was a worry, of course, I hated to think of her being disadvantaged in any way, especially at such a crucial stage in her development. I knew how important it was for teenage girls to have the right image – and, more importantly – the same image. I worried she might be bullied or left out because she looked differently to all her friends. But Jodey being Jodey, she didn't seem to let it bother her too much. Like most girls her age, she didn't look too far ahead and her friends just accepted her the way she was.

Her mood swings and her tantrums continued; made worse, I suspected, by the maelstrom of adolescent hormones bubbling alongside. Sometimes, her outbursts left me speechless. She was like a human roller-coaster; up, down and upside down. I never knew quite what to expect next.

Donna and Jamie were both placid and even-tempered, they worked hard at school, and I'd had no problems at all with either of them. But that just made Jodey's issues all the more perplexing and confusing.

"I don't know where you get it from!" I used to say to her.

And yet, day to day, her behaviour wasn't something that usually dominated my thoughts. We accepted and loved Jodey just exactly for who she was, and those sparkling and unexpected acts of kindness, like visiting me each day in hospital, or comforting Jamie when he had a nightmare, more than made up for her meltdowns.

Besides, in many ways, she was a typical teenage girl. Her problems certainly did not control or even overshadow her life. She and her best friend, Debbie, were insepar-able. In the nice weather, they loved to sunbathe outside, together with the other girls on the estate. They'd spread a blanket out and line up Jodey's dolls. Even now, she was impervious to the other girls ribbing her about her dolls. She didn't care one bit.

As they got older, they'd take a cassette player outside, and paint each other with garish bright green and blue eyeshadows and pearly pink lipstick. In-between the dancing and the singing there was lots of screeching every time someone brought out a compact mirror for a make-over moment. And of course, there was always a line of little children following Jodey, like faithful ducklings.

"You're the perfect Mummy duck," I smiled.

She and Debbie loved most of the chart music, but they were crazy about Madonna. For Jodey's 13th birthday, I had bought her pod shoes, with tags on the laces, and she wore them with different brightly coloured socks. She draped herself in lace and silver jewellery and layers of chains and silver bangles, just like Madonna. She squeezed lemon juice into her hair and wore it in a high, jaunty, ponytail.

"Wow! You look just like Madonna!" I teased her. "You could be twins!"

Each afternoon after school, she and Debbie would run upstairs and put a tape on full blast. I'd groan as they belted out *Material Girl* and *Papa Don't Preach* down a plastic microphone, and the living room light fitting would judder in protest as they danced away, rehearsing the moves they'd picked up from Madonna's latest video.

"Can I bleach my hair like Madonna?" Jodey asked me, her bright blue eyes wide and, she hoped, persuasive. "Please Mam, can I?"

"No," I said shortly. "You're too young. Forget it."

There was one occasion, a Saturday morning, when I gave Jodey money to go to the hairdressers for a trim. Debbie was booked in alongside her. When they arrived home afterwards, I looked up from my ironing and did a double take.

"Your hair isn't even straight!" I gasped, staring at Jodey's fringe in horror. "What on earth have they done to you?"

Jodey shrugged; she didn't even seem too concerned. I switched my attention to Debbie.

"Your hair is wonky too!" I exclaimed. "What's going on?"

Debbie was equally tight-lipped and I was beginning to smell a rat. It wasn't until I grabbed my coat, ready to go and complain in person to the hairdresser, that they caved in. Suppressing her giggles, Jodey confessed that they had pocketed the money to buy the new Madonna album instead, and had cut each other's hair.

"Well you two girls look like you've had a fight with a lawnmower," I retorted. "So it serves you right."

Eric was living only two miles away and he was still very hands-on with the kids. He and Jodey had a good relationship but, like any teenager, she would play Eric and I off against each other, stoking up trouble between us to cover up her own misdemeanours. Donna and Jamie seemed to have adapted more easily to our separation than Jodey. As expected, she was the one who found it a challenge.

Through friends, I met a new partner, Allan Dove, who was a welder. We began dating and it felt like a whole new chapter for me. I had been lonely on my own with the kids, and suddenly here was someone who put me first, for a change. Allan made me really happy. He booked holidays and nights out for us; something I felt I'd missed out on in my marriage, because I'd gone straight from teenager to wife and mother, with no interim period. Eric and I had become adults when we were little more than children ourselves. With Allan, I felt like I was making up for all that lost time. He whisked me away to Devon and Cornwall, and he took me on a canal boat trip which I loved. So when he proposed, I was over the moon.

"Yes," I beamed. "I'd love to get married."

Our big day was set for June 17, 1989. But in the run-up to the wedding, Jodey really started playing up. Her flare-ups seemed to get worse, or perhaps it was just because, at age 14, she had got much taller and bigger, and when she threw a tantrum, it took over the whole house. The foundations themselves seemed to shake, and the noise was deafening. There was a crack in the plaster over the living room door which inched along, each time she slammed it in temper. As it grew longer, the gap between Jodey and I widened.

"I can't cope with this," I told her despairingly. "It's getting to us all."

She was smoking too; I could smell it on her clothes. The pocket money she'd once saved for dolls' clothes and then for Madonna records was now being wasted on cigarettes. It was a predictable sequence of events, and she was no different than any other teenager in many respects. But it was still upsetting. And I'd had no real problems with Donna throughout her teens, so this was something new for me. At first, I tried to tell myself that Jodey was simply being a stroppy adolescent and that the mass of hormones, along with the outbursts, would diffuse in time. But I slowly realised, just like the childhood tantrums, that this behaviour stemmed from something concrete and deep-rooted. This wasn't a phase, and it wasn't just hormones or teenage rebellion; this was part of who Jodey was.

"I want to help you, Jode," I said. "But I don't know what to do."

I made an appointment with the GP and he listened carefully as I described Jodey's challenging behaviour. But as I continued, I could tell he wasn't really taking me seriously. He began rolling his eyes and making little quips about teenagers. Then, he stood up, opened the door, and said:

"I wouldn't worry, I'm sure she'll grow out of it."

I had heard those words so often and they made me feel like screaming. I felt like I was running out of ideas, like something had to give. So when Eric suggested that Jodey could go and stay with him and his new partner for a while, I jumped at the chance, with some relief.

"Change of scene might be just what she needs," he told me.

I knew I would miss her. But I also knew she needed to get back on track. I would still see her every day, and she was pleased too, to spend some time with her dad.

In June 1989, Allan and I were married at Stockton-on-Tees Register Office. I was 35 years old; more than twice the age I'd been at my first wedding, and it was yet another reminder of how young Eric and I had been. Perhaps we had never really stood a chance.

Jodey seemed to enjoy the ceremony, she wore a new dress and afterwards, at the reception at the working men's club, she danced all night. Every time the coloured lights of the disco zoomed round to her, she was smiling, and her face was luminous with happiness. It struck me that there were no in-betweens with Jodey, there was no equilibrium. Like the little girl in the nursery rhyme, she was a girl of extremes; when she was good, she was very, very good, but when she was bad she was horrid! As I watched her dance, I hoped, more than anything, that life would bring her calmness and stability.

\* \* \*

One morning, around a month after the wedding, Eric called me in a panic.

"Jodey isn't here," he said. "Doesn't look as though her bed's been slept in. Is she with you?"

"No," I replied, my heart sinking.

We called around her friends and we tried the school too, but nobody had seen her. She was due to break up for summer in the next few days and so her teachers had presumed we had perhaps gone away.

"Where can she be?" I fretted.

The signs were all there. She had taken her favourite blue handbag, she had left her room tidy, and her bed was made. Hard as it was, I had to accept that this was no accident, and that she had probably run away. Deep down, we had been half expecting this; her behaviour had been spiralling. But it was nevertheless a huge shock. The stark truth was stomach-churning. My daughter was missing, she was actually missing, and we had no idea where she was, or even if she was safe.

"We'll find her," Eric said, with a confidence I just couldn't share.

I called in at work to make my excuses and all that morning, I trawled the local parks and shops, looking for my daughter. I didn't want to involve the police; I didn't want to make this into a more serious issue than it already was. I knew also that she would be embarrassed and annoyed if I called the police, and that might just drive her even further away. Besides, I felt sure that she was hiding out with a friend somewhere. I felt certain she would surface, in her own time. And yet, as the hours ticked by, and there was no news, I became frantic. I imagined her being hurt or assaulted. I worried she might have been in an accident. Had she been abducted – or worse? The possibilities burned through my mind, one by one. Where was she? Eventually, as evening came, I felt I had no choice.

"My daughter's missing, she's 15, but she's never run away before," I told the officer who took my call. "I've tried all her friends. I've looked everywhere. I don't know what else to do."

The police took a description and promised to call round to collect a photo. But I had no sooner put the phone down than I heard the front door opening.

"Jodey!" I yelled, flying into the hallway. "We've been worried sick!"

I'd been prepared to give her a piece of my mind but seeing her standing there, still so much a child, vulnerable and beautiful, I was awash with relief and love.

"You're safe now," I said, burying my face in her hair. "It's all that matters."

She'd stayed with a friend, she told me. She insisted she had always planned to come back home.

"You can't just run off whenever the fancy takes you," I said firmly, as I cooked her sausage and mash. "Can't you see what that does to us?"

"Oh Mam stop fussing," she said. "It's no big deal. Any more sausages?"

Again, Jodey was swinging between two irreconcilable psyches. She had endless patience, of course, for the children she babysat. And yet she seemed to have a complete lack of empathy for the strain she was causing in her family. In tears, I waited until Jodey had flounced back out of the house to see her dad, before calling my best friend, Jan Scott, to pour my heart out.

"Typical teenager," she said. "They all put their parents through hell. We did it ourselves, back in the day!"

I wanted so much for that to be true. But deep down, I knew it was more serious. It was less than a week before

Jodey disappeared again; somehow sneaking out, just before bedtime. Again, I called the police and tried all her friends. Nothing. Through the night, I paced the living room. I didn't sleep a wink. It didn't help at all that this wasn't the first time, if anything, I felt even worse. I felt she was tempting fate, using up her chances, and that something was bound to happen to her. The night felt endless. At times, I was furious with her, bubbling over with anger. The fact that she would do this again, knowing how much I worried, was unthinkable. I stood at the front window, scanning the deserted street, watching and waiting. And as the first light of dawn streaked through an inky sky, I was suddenly frozen with fear.

"Where is she?" I pleaded out loud.

The thought of my little Jodey out there, so streetwise with her Madonna necklaces and her secret cigarettes, yet still so very much a child, was terrifying beyond measure. By 5am, I was ready to forgive anything, for the reward of seeing my daughter's beautiful face; her cheeky smile, her brilliant blue eyes, so full of enthusiasm. It was after breakfast when Eric called me to say she had turned up at his place. By now, I was dropping with exhaustion.

"I'll let the police know," I told him weakly.

Another few weeks later, and Jodey vanished once again. I was reaching breaking-point, existing on my nerves, with very little sleep. By now, the police were treating her as a habitual runaway.

"She's only 15," I reminded them. "Shouldn't you be out looking for her?"

I felt her disappearances were being downgraded and taken less seriously. It was frustrating; she was still a child. She was *my* child. She was never away for more than one night, usually staying with a bunch of new friends who we didn't know. But for me, that was scant comfort. I needed to know where she was, every night.

"One of these days, something bad will happen to you and nobody will know," I told Jodey. "The police won't listen. I don't know half of what you're up to. You're playing with fire."

But Jodey didn't listen. Like most teenagers, she thought she was invincible. She just didn't think of the dangers. She continued to go missing, sometimes only for a few hours here and there, but it got to the point where I was afraid of letting her out of my sight. Eric was beside himself with worry, as I was. And poor Donna probably grew up more quickly than she wanted to; I enlisted her to help with searches and to grill Jodey's friends and classmates each time she went missing. I asked Donna to memorise the contents of Jodey's bedroom and tell me what was missing each time she vanished. As her big sister, and only 18 herself, she would probably far rather have colluded with Jodey, or at least have not been so involved. But Donna was responsible and level-headed, she had been that way since she was small, and she did what she could to help me. Jamie, though, was four years younger than Jodey, and he idolised her. He worried terribly when she was missing and he hated the inevitable stress when she showed up again, as Eric and I tried – and failed – to find a suitable punishment to deter her. And all of this, of course, served only to isolate and alienate Jodey even more. She felt as though we were all siding against her, as though she was on her own.

"Might as well run away," she complained. "I'm always in trouble at home."

"You're in trouble because you keep running off," I said, trying hard to keep my voice level. "Can't you see that?"

She shrugged and turned away. I couldn't understand why she was behaving like this. Again, there was that nagging voice inside me that told me there had to be more to this. I felt there was a missing piece. Jodey was impulsive and naïve, yes, but she was also caring and affectionate. She had a good heart. I had always thought that she and I were close, that we were friends as well as mother and daughter. And in spite of our divorce, Eric and I were loving parents. We did our best. So what was going wrong? In desperation, I made another appointment with the GP, who again tried to dismiss Jodey's troubles as a teenage phase.

"I insist on her seeing a specialist," I pleaded. "Please. A psychologist, a psychiatrist, anyone who deals with adolescent behaviour. I am begging you."

The GP sucked in his breath and nodded, but warned:

"The referral will take some time. And even then, don't expect any clear-cut answers."

I spoke to Jodey's teachers too and inevitably, soon after, social services got involved. It was a moment I'd been dreading and yet I knew we needed help.

"Jodey please, listen to me," I said. "If you don't start behaving, you will end up in care."

I had said to frighten her, to shock her to her senses. But Jodey barked out a short laugh.

"Good," she snapped. "I'd rather be in care. That suits me just fine."

My heart sank. It was just like her to call my bluff. And sure enough, when the support worker turned up to see her, Jodey was waiting with her bag packed.

"I'm ready," she said. "I'm sick of this place."

The impact of those words was devastating. I felt a physical pain in my chest, as though someone had dropped a brick on me. My own daughter, announcing to the world that she'd rather live in care than live with her own family! I didn't even know what I'd done wrong. My cheeks burned with shame as Jodey sauntered down the path with her big Madonna bow in the back of her hair. Her bangles jangled, fainter and fainter still, as she pulled her carry case along behind her. The support worker shook her head sympathetically.

"I don't think she'll be away long somehow," she said, with a wry smile. "Teenagers can be very testing."

But that was no comfort. I watched the car drive away and I felt as though I had been torn in two. Part of me was in that car, with Jodey, pleading with her to reconsider. And part of me was stuck at home; rejected and redundant. I tried to dam back the tears, but it was impossible; they burst through and streamed down my face.

"It'll wake her up, it might do her good," Donna told me. "She'll realise she has a family who loves her."

I nodded miserably.

"She's immature," Jan consoled me. "She doesn't think things through. I bet she's already regretting it."

Again, the words offered little solace. I imagined the care home as a great Victorian orphanage, with thin, miserable duvets and iron-willed wardens, neither offering much warmth. The next day, I went straight after work to the address the social workers had given me. To my surprise, it was an ordinary looking family home, and inside, I found Jodey sitting at a dining table. Her face lit up, despite herself, when she spotted me.

"I've brought you some treats," I said, emptying out my bag. "I wasn't sure if you'd get enough to eat or if they'd cook the stuff you like."

"I'm fine," she insisted, but she stuffed the snacks into her pockets all the same.

It turned out there were only two other teenagers living there, along with support workers, and the house was reassuringly ordinary; welcoming and warm. But when I was leaving, the emotion overpowered me again and Jodey's eyes swam with tears too.

"You don't belong here," I sobbed. "I wish you could see that."

All the way home, on the bus, I was inconsolable. Everyone had told me it was for the best, that it would do her good, that it was the short, sharp shock Jodey needed. And yet, as I gazed out of the windows, at the dreary lines of shops and houses, the bare and painful facts glared back at me. My daughter, my own daughter, was in the care of social services. She had a perfectly good home. So what kind of mother did that make me? I felt as though everyone around me on the bus was whispering and gossiping and passing judgement.

'Daughter in care, daughter in care…'

The words ran around my mind to the shunting rhythm of the bus.

'In care, in care, in care…'

It might just as well have been branded across my forehead. Where had I gone wrong?

I visited Jodey again the next day, and the next, taking more treats and a few home comforts. I'd noticed she'd left a Madonna cassette tape in her bedroom, so I took that for her too. I was allowed to visit every day, after work, and I found myself counting the minutes until I could see her. Ten days in, a social worker took me aside.

"Jodey has asked if she can come home," she said.

Feeling my legs buckle, I almost folded over in sheer relief. She had come to her senses at last. After just two weeks in the care home, she was coming back to her family, back where she belonged. The social worker drove her home, and I wrapped my arms around her, drinking in the smell of her hair, the feel of her cheek on mine, and vowing never ever to let her go. That brief separation had, I think, done Jodey some good. As before, she split her time between Eric's place and mine. Donna by now had moved into her own flat, and Jodey spent lots of time with her too. Our problems were by no means over, I had never expected that, but Jodey did at least stop running away. She still had mood swings and meltdowns, and the concerns over her behaviour ran like an uneasy undercurrent through our lives. But I managed those outbursts the best I could. Jodey was home, she was safe, and nothing else mattered.

# 4

# 'I'm Pregnant. Again!'

In October 1990, Jodey celebrated her 16<sup>th</sup> birthday. Like any teenage girl, her life revolved around clothes, make-up and jewellery, and for her birthday I gave her money, along with a few nick-nacks. We celebrated with a cake and a little party at home. She had lots of friends and they all came too with cards and gifts.

"This is going to be a good year for you," I beamed. "I can feel it."

I believed, or perhaps I wanted to believe, that we had come through the worst of her problems. Certainly, I wanted to push that dreadful dark period of her running away firmly into the past.

"I hope you're right, Mam," Jodey grinned, as she tried on a new pair of earrings that Donna had bought her.

A month later, into November, the weather went really cold, and it felt as though winter was setting in. Jodey was spending a few days with me, and I had made a chicken casserole for tea.

"This will warm you up," I smiled, as I passed the plates around.

Jodey was uncharacteristically quiet, pushing her food around the plate, but I sensed that she was itching to tell me something. She was restless and twitchy, almost as though she was working on keeping her mouth from racing ahead without permission from her brain. I waited until Jamie had gone upstairs and Allan was settled in front of the TV, and then I whispered:

"What's the matter with you, Jode? I can read you like a book."

Her face was a peculiar mixture of anxiety and excitement.

"Well," she began. "I've something to tell you, Mam. I'm having a baby."

Her eyes met mine and for a moment, the silence felt sharp and tense, as she waited for my reaction. Instinctively, I wanted to scream and cry; she was too young, too immature, she didn't have her own home or a job. She was still at school for goodness' sake! We had only just got over the trauma of her running away from home, and now she was going to be a mother herself! I hadn't even known she had a serious boyfriend. I had no idea. But then, in a flash, I rewound 19 years, and there I was, standing in front of my own mother, terrified and alone, but at the same time so thrilled to be carrying a new life inside me.

"Come here," I said, arms outstretched, eyes shining with tears. "It'll be fine love. I'm here for you, whatever you decide."

Jodey took a step back, out of my arms, her face glowing defiantly, her blue eyes sparkling with a familiar determination.

"I've already made up my mind. I'm keeping the baby. No way I'm getting rid of it, don't even think about it."

I allowed myself a smile. I recognised that obstinance, that grit. I'd said those same words myself when I was carrying Donna. Already, weeks into her pregnancy, Jodey was behaving like a mother, protecting her chick, holding her close. And yes, she was young, and gosh, she had a lot to learn. But she was also, and I had felt it since she was a little girl herself, born to be a mother. She'd be a natural. I was sure of that.

"I'll support you," I promised again. "And I think this baby will be the making of you."

Jodey soon brought her new boyfriend home to meet me.

"Mam, this is Karl," she smiled.

I could see straightaway that they were well-matched. Karl was as calm and laid-back as Jodey was headstrong and whirlwind. Most importantly, he seemed to adore her. Though Karl was only young himself, just eight months older than Jodey, he had a strong sense of family and responsibility and as the weeks passed, I realised that he was a true keeper.

"You've got a diamond there," I told Jodey.

"I know," she winked, rubbing her bump. "I'm so happy, Mam. I've got it all."

I saved every spare penny I could and together she and I went round the charity shops and the markets, picking up tiny items of clothing and baby equipment. Soon we had a pram and a cot waiting in my cramped hallway.

"I just can't wait," I beamed, crossing off another week on the calendar.

The pregnancy went well, despite some back pain, and just as I had expected, Jodey breezed through it. Despite the problems we'd had with her, she had never been a drinker and she didn't go out partying or clubbing, so it was not a big sacrifice for her to give up her social life. Instead, she looked after herself and her bump and she started reading in the evenings. Typically, she loved true stories about children; tear-jerking tales of orphans or of lost children.

"These books make me cry, but I love them," she told me. "I should have started reading years ago."

I went with her to every antenatal appointment and scan. When we found out she was carrying a boy, we were over the moon. As her stomach swelled, and the date drew nearer, we grew more and more excited. One day early in June 1991, we went out shopping for some final bits and bobs for the baby. Jodey had just a month left in her pregnancy.

"Let's get more bibs, and more vests," I decided. "Honestly pet, you can never have too many. You wouldn't believe how many changes of clothes they need when they're tiny."

At the bus stop, on our way home, Jodey suddenly grabbed my arm and groaned loudly.

"Oh no," she gasped. "Mam, my waters have gone!"

I looked down and there it was; a small puddle on the pavement; the first sign that my grandson was on his way. He was four weeks early, but I tried to not think about that. I didn't want Jodey to panic. Donna's house was nearer than mine so we hobbled off to her street, as fast as we could, with Jodey clutching onto my hand. She seemed all at once like a child again; looking to me for advice and help; her eyes stretched wide with fear. In that same moment as she was about to become a mother, she needed her own mother more than ever.

"Donna!" I yelled, rapping on the door. "Quick, Donna!"

Donna had a baby daughter of her own, and the moment she saw Jodey, leaning on the garden fence and breathing heavily, she knew exactly what was happening.

"Let's get her inside, I'll call an ambulance," she said. "Breathe, Jodey, breathe."

The paramedics arrived within minutes, and Jodey and I were both whisked off to North Tees Hospital. By now it was early evening, and Jodey's contractions were stop-start. As the hours passed, she became worn out and frustrated.

"I'm here," I reassured her, my hand on hers.

But it was hard watching her suffer.

"It'll all be worth it," I promised her. "Just squeeze my hand."

After a full 24 hours of labour, she finally held her baby boy, David, in her arms. Despite being born early, he weighed 7lbs and was absolutely perfect. The joy and the love shone from Jodey; it seemed to illuminate her whole face.

"I can't believe he's mine," she kept saying. "I just can't believe it. I'm the luckiest girl in the world."

In the weeks that followed, Jodey settled into motherhood as though the role had been specially created for her. Even though she was so young, she didn't complain once about missing out on shopping trips or parties with her pals. She hardly seemed to notice what her friends were up to. Now, all that mattered to her was Karl and her new baby son. And yet neither was she over-protective or over-anxious. She didn't crowd baby David at all; she knew when to cuddle him and she also knew when he needed to be left to sleep. She seemed, already, so settled and so confident as a mother.

"I always imagined that being a mam would be the best thing ever," she confided. "And actually, it's even better than that!"

* * *

Jodey left school that summer and soon after, she was called in for a hospital appointment, following on from the referral by our GP. I could hardly believe someone was finally about to address the behavioural difficulties she'd been having throughout her childhood. Together, we waited expectantly for the consultant to speak.

"You have bipolar disorder and emotionally unstable personality disorder, also borderline personality disorder," he told Jodey. "I know this will come as a shock, but I hope it will help to explain why you have faced so many obstacles in life."

My mouth fell open. This was not what I had been expecting. I had been preparing myself to be fobbed off and sent home with platitudes. And I had never even heard of these conditions. But, as he explained the signs, everything, in that instant, began to make sense. Sufferers displayed dramatic and unpredictable behaviour and they experienced severe mood swings, he said. They could be overly emotional and impulsive, and they had feelings of emptiness and worthlessness. I thought back to Jodey's tantrum in the GP surgery, of her outbursts at home which seemed to spring from nowhere, and this described her perfectly. It was more than the final piece of a jigsaw; it was as though someone had drawn back a thick veil and I was seeing my daughter clearly and properly for the first time. The doctor also said:

"Someone with these conditions might find it difficult to maintain stable relationships."

I remembered Jodey's phase of running away followed by her brief spell in care. Again, it made perfect sense. This doctor seemed to know my daughter better than many of her family and friends.

I reached out to squeeze Jodey's hand and saw her face was pale and blank. My heart was so sore for her. As much as the diagnosis was a relief, it was equally very distressing. On the one hand, the fact that her problems had a medical origin was in some ways a comfort; we at least knew that there was a logical reason for her erratic behaviour. There was the promise that she might receive help and support too. There was the assurance that she was not alone. This was the confirmation I had sought since she was just a little girl. She was not a naughty child. She was ill. I could have wept with gratitude.

And yet, the label was damning. It threw her whole future into doubt. I had always suspected, always known, if I was honest, that there was something different about my daughter. But this diagnosis sounded so serious and official. All through Jodey's life, I had oscillated between trying to make doctors recognise her problems and trying to pretend that she was just the same as everyone else. I wanted her to fit in with the rest of society, I didn't want her to be different, because of the trouble it would cause her. Now, with this diagnosis, she was being marked out and marginalised. I felt she might just as well have had it scrawled in marker pen across her face.

"I still don't know what it all means," Jodey admitted, as we left the hospital. "I didn't really understand what the doctor said, Mam."

And that was part of the tragedy; her condition itself was preventing her from being able to process what exactly it meant for her. More than anything, she was confused.

"We don't need to know what it means," I said eventually, slipping my arm around her. "You're still you. You're still Jodey. Nothing has changed. Just remember that."

I didn't know whether my approach was right or wrong. All I could do was follow my instinct, as a mother, and offer her the love and reassurance she needed. We came away from the appointment with a prescription and Jodey began the course that same week. But the medication did not agree with her and caused a whole raft of unpleasant side-effects.

"This is awful, Mam," she said. "I feel worse than ever."

We requested another appointment and were told it would be trial and error until her doctors got the prescription right. She would simply have to grit her teeth and put up with it. When David was a couple of months old, Jodey and Karl got their own place; a little flat not far from me. Jodey had always been creative, even at school, it had showed in the way she matched her dollies' outfits and, later, her own. Now with her own home, she showed a real eye for interior design and decoration, and even though she didn't have much money, she made it look lovely with new curtains and cushions and little lamps; small touches that made all the difference. She got a part-time job, in a charity shop, and her boss quickly realised what a flair she had for design. Soon she was in charge of arranging the window dressing. I babysat David whilst they were working, and often I would push the pram past the shop and stop to admire her handiwork.

"Look at your mam's window display," I cooed to David. "Isn't she clever?"

As well as making Jodey so happy, Karl had slotted so well into the dynamics of our family too. He got on great with Donna and Jamie, and he was like a second son to me and Eric. So when Jodey burst through the door one day wearing a sparkling engagement ring, I was over the moon. Their wedding was booked for the same day as her 18th birthday, October 16 1992. It was to be a double celebration.

"We'll have the best party," I vowed.

Jodey was the first of my children to get married and I wanted to make it really special. Of course, we didn't have much money but that didn't matter. As usual, Jodey's only concern was that the younger guests would be catered for, with party games and balloons and kids' snacks. It seemed to me that she was inviting more children than adults! At that time, I was working as a barmaid in the local pub, The George and Dragon, so I managed to wangle the function room for free. I offered to do the buffet myself too. My brother, Norman, chipped in with an offer to video the event. It was a wedding on a very short shoestring, but that didn't make it any the less exciting. Middlesbrough Register Office was booked for the afternoon, and we spent the morning helping Jodey into her wedding dress, curling her long fair hair and applying and reapplying her make-up. She had no nerves at all. She was so sure of Karl, and so confident that she was doing the right thing and it was lovely to see. As we left the house, Jodey piped up, on the spur of the moment:

"I'm starving! Anyone for the chippy?"

My jaw dropped as she marched into a nearby chip shop, resplendent in her bridal gown and veil, and placed an order for fish and chips.

"Jodey!" I shrieked. "Look at the time. We're running late as it is!"

I was stunned. Yet in another way, it was not at all shocking. Jodey did things her way and I knew that by now. She and Donna emerged from the shop a few minutes later, balancing trays of chips along with their bouquets, and I dissolved into giggles.

"Only you, Jodey-Podey," I said, shaking my head. "You're one of a kind, alright."

The wedding day was fantastic; little David was so cute in his page-boy suit. That night, as I drifted off to sleep, I realised that for the first time, possibly in her entire life, I was not worried about Jodey. I was pleased for her, proud of her, even a little envious, as she began a new chapter of her life. But I was not worried. I felt lighter and clearer and more confident than I had for years. It felt like this was Jodey's time, at last.

\* \* \*

Jodey had always wanted a big family and so it was no surprise to anyone when she announced her second pregnancy soon after the wedding.

"Brilliant news!" I smiled.

She was closely monitored by the hospital, and, with her doctors' approval, she didn't take her medication whilst she was pregnant. This pregnancy was a little more difficult because of the curvature in her spine and the drop in her shoulder. As her bump grew, she complained a little of aches and pains.

In time, she gave birth to a daughter, Louise, and the following year she had a son, Simon. Jodey and Karl moved with their little family to Hartlepool, and they juggled looking after their young family whilst both working in the same nursing home. They were busy and happy, full of the energy and the plans of new parents. In those years, I saw them mainly at weekends. We'd get together for a Saturday night takeaway or a Sunday lunch, to fit round their work shifts. Shortly after Simon was born, Jodey's back pain worsened, and she found herself back at the hospital. She was told that carrying three babies, and especially so close together, had aggravated her existing troubles.

"I've got to have surgery, Mam," she said. "I'm dreading it."

"If it helps with the pain, it's worth it," I said. "I'll help out with the kids, don't fret."

My marriage to Allan had hit a rocky patch and, much as I adored my grandchildren, they were also a welcome distraction from my problems at home too. I was only too happy to look after them. Soon after, Jodey had surgery to remove a disc from her back. For a few days, she was sore and slow, but then she seemed to bounce back pretty quickly. She insisted that it had been successful and that the discomfort was no more than a niggle.

"I'm fine," she told me, smiling as she hoisted a baby onto each hip.

But I saw the way she frowned and winced, and I knew, like a typically selfless parent, she was pushing her own needs to the bottom of the list. Sometimes, I'd catch her biting her lip and rubbing her back and I knew her problems could not be smothered forever. On Jodey's 21$^{st}$ birthday, in October 1995, I threw a surprise party for her at home, decorating the windows with balloons and banners. When she walked in, we all burst out from behind the sofa and the curtains, and yelled:

"Surprise! Happy Birthday!"

Jodey, with a little one on either side and one in the pram too, had the widest smile. Despite the sleep deprivation and the chaos, and the frequent twinges of pain, she was radiant. It was just as we had always predicted; motherhood suited her perfectly. We played Madonna and Michael Jackson records all afternoon and Jodey, glass of wine in hand, danced around the living room with Donna.

"It's like turning back time," I smiled. "I can see you two at 14 and 16, all over again."

Jodey loved to dance. But she was most content, as usual, sitting on the floor with the little ones, playing pass the parcel and pin the tail on the donkey. She was 21, yet still a child at heart. Afterwards, she and Karl moved to a bigger house and in January 1997, they had a second little girl, Lisa. And when Lisa was only a few weeks old, Jodey rang me.

"You'll not believe this, Mam," she said. "I'm pregnant. Again!"

"Wow!" I gasped. "You're popping these babies out like peas!"

A new baby, a new life was always good news, no matter what the circumstances. She and I both believed that. But even so, I was a little apprehensive and wondered how she would cope.

"I'll be fine," she promised me. "I'm thrilled."

The night before she was due to have her first scan, I had a vivid dream, and in it, Jodey had given birth to twins with rosy cheeks and cherubic smiles. She was walking down the street with one baby on either arm. All around her, in the air, plump babies fluttered and flew, flapping their chubby arms like little birds, some perching on her shoulder, some landing on her head or her arm.

"I'm the mother hen, Mam," she smiled in the dream. "Just like you always said."

The dream was so realistic that when I awoke, I almost expected to see a flock of babies floating past my bedroom window. I called Jodey before breakfast to wish her luck with her scan, and to tell her about my dream.

"Honestly, clear as day, you were walking down the road with twins," I told her.

"You're crackers," she chuckled.

By now, I was working in a butcher's shop, just as I had when I was younger. And that afternoon, as I was packaging up lamb chops, Jodey came racing into the shop, bundling through the astonished customers with her pram, right to the front of the queue.

"Guess what!" she announced breathlessly. "It's twins! You were right! Your dream was spot on!"

As word went down the queue the customers began cheering and clapping and congratulating Jodey and me. I was as stunned as they were. I had never for a moment expected it to come true.

"Mam, we need you to dream up the lottery numbers for next week," Jodey said, with a wink. "And we'll all be rich!"

The twins were due in October 1997, meaning Jodey would give birth to three babies in the space of only ten months. Again, I had concerns about how she'd manage, especially with the soreness in her back. But she waved my niggles away.

"I love babies, you know that," she said. "The more, the merrier."

Not for the first time, it struck me as curious that Jodey struggled with so many everyday situations, like sitting still in an appointment or following a set of instructions. And yet, when it came to children, she had endless patience and ability. Most people would be overawed by the prospect of having six children under the age of six. But Jodey sailed through it all. She saw each child as a gift. The twins, Tommy and Tasha, came along that October, and they were perfect. Jodey had a natural birth and recovered quickly at home. She was in her element with her brood. I cannot remember a single time I visited when she didn't have a baby in her arms and a toddler at her feet. She was always on the go.

"Pass me that nappy, Mam, and could you pop a bottle on for me? I'm glad you're here, we're just about to sing nursery rhymes!"

That winter, Jodey picked up a stubborn cold, not unusual given the bugs that little ones pass around, but this one just wouldn't clear up. At first, we paid little attention to it. Then, I bought her tonics and vitamins to try, and I took the twins overnight so that she could get a good night's sleep. Yet nothing helped and her chest rattled and wheezed all through the cold winter months. Eventually, her GP diagnosed her with pleurisy and sent her to The University

Hospital of North Tees. By now, she could barely breathe. I went straight to the hospital and found Jodey, translucently pale and gasping for breath, in bed. Her eyes were cloudy with fear.

"Do you think I'm going to die?" she rasped, snatching at each little pocket of air.

I shook my head firmly, but I was privately very concerned. My sister, Maureen, worked as a nurse at the same hospital and she promised to keep a close eye on Jodey for me.

"Call me, night or day," I said to Maureen.

It was another full week, before Maureen announced: "I think she's over the worst now."

Two weeks on, Jodey was allowed home from hospital, but even then, she was weak and short of breath. It was a reminder, if any was needed, that her health was brittle and fragile. Her disabilities, though she didn't like to recognise them as such, lurked in the background, like ghosts. As much as she tried to ignore them, and push them away, they would never completely disappear.

\* \* \*

By the spring, Jodey had made a good recovery and she was kept very busy at home. I called round to see her growing family every other day, usually tripping on a toy truck in the garden or a headless doll in the hallway. If the windows were open, I could hear the laughter and the bickering all the way down the street. It was one of the best sounds ever. The washing machine whirred all day every day, and Karl was always cooking. Jodey was often painting or colouring at the dining table or dressing dollies up from her spot on the living floor. She was in her element. In addition to her own brood, she'd often child-mind for neighbours or friends, either as a favour, or to earn a bit of extra money.

"As if you haven't enough children of your own!" I exclaimed.

But Jodey just shrugged. For her, there was no such thing as too many children. I helped out, bringing shopping and running errands, and I did the school run sometimes too. Allan and I had divorced by this time, and so I had more time and freedom to be with my grandchildren, which was just as well, because when the twins were two years old, Jodey had another daughter, Helen. And afterwards, she came to a decision.

"I'm going to apply to college," she told me. "I'd like to be a midwife. I could be qualified and ready to work by the time the little ones are starting school."

It would be a challenge, returning to education. I knew she regretted not stretching herself at school, but she'd had undiagnosed behavioural and psychological issues, and of course she had been pregnant in that final year. The odds were well and truly stacked against her. Now, she was older and more mature, and she had the benefit of diagnosis and medication. Besides, bringing babies into the world was something she felt passionately about. I knew she would give it her all. She applied to Middlesbrough College to begin a foundation course and was accepted and advised to wait for a start date. She saw her GP too and was referred for sterilisation surgery.

"I love my babies, but I can tell my body is starting to crumble," she said. "I think seven will have to be enough for me."

"Seven would be enough to finish most people off," I laughed. "I think you've made the right decision."

Jodey was booked in at the hospital for her operation, early in 2000. But less than a week before her operation, she called me, and I could almost hear the giggle in her voice before she spoke. I knew, somehow, exactly what she was about to say.

"You won't believe it," she began.

"Let me guess," I interrupted. "You're having another one!"

"Yes" she squealed. "It feels like I only have to sit on the same sofa as Karl and I'm pregnant again!"

The following month, I went along with her to the scan, because Karl was working. The sonographer frowned a little as a fuzzy image appeared on screen, and then she started to smile.

"Look at this!" she said.

She pointed and there was no further explanation needed. There, on the monitor, were two tiny heartbeats, flashing boldly, like beacons from another universe.

"Twins!" I gulped. "Again!"

Jodey and I looked at each other in shock before she started to laugh.

"Oh Jode," I grinned. "This could only happen to you!"

Her studies, like the sterilisation, had to be postponed, perhaps indefinitely. And yet there was no sense of disappointment or regret. Jodey couldn't wait to be a mother again.

"I feel like it happened for a reason," she said. "Maybe I'm meant to be a mam and not a midwife, and that's fine by me. I think raising children is the most important job in the world. It's a privilege."

But as the months passed, and her bump grew, I noticed Jodey was struggling more and more. She was stooping awkwardly, and her shoulders were becoming more lop-sided. She couldn't pick the children up without grimacing in agony.

"I'm in a lot of pain with my back," she admitted. "But there's not much the doctors can do until the babies arrive. I'm just going to have to put up with it. I can't even have a painkiller whilst I'm pregnant."

The doctors had already warned that she might need more surgery on her back. But for the past few years she had been so busy with motherhood that she had barely given her own health a second thought. Now though, I feared the delay was catching up with her, and the strain on her body was finally starting to show.

Jodey gave birth to beautiful twin boys, Christopher and Cory, in November 2000. Now, a mother of nine children, all under the age of ten, Jodey had everything she had ever wanted. But as I watched her hobble around the house, her face drawn and shot through with pain, I wondered and worried at the price she had paid.

\* \* \*

With nine children, and only one full-time wage, Jodey naturally had to be careful with her money and making it last each week was something of a magic trick, and something I remembered myself, all too well. Yet I'd had only three children to look after, and she had three times that. She shopped all year round for Christmas and birthday presents and there was a little room at the back of their house, which was piled high, floor to ceiling, in anticipation of the next event. Every year, she and Karl had a huge Christmas tree, and the house was decorated with lights and Christmas signs. Jodey's flair for design showed in every room, and the kids' bedrooms, especially, were beautifully decorated. Jamie was a talented artist and Jodey had asked him to design murals of their favourite film and cartoon characters. Despite piles of toys and books and shoes around the house, it was always sparkling clean and tidy. On such a tight budget, Jodey had the place looking like a little palace.

"You should have been a fashion designer," I told her. "Or you could be on that telly programme where they renovate houses."

"I'd rather be a mam," she replied.

By now, they were living in a four-bedroom house in Thornaby, Stockton-on-Tees, and they had converted the downstairs dining room into a fifth bedroom, so there was plenty of space for the kids. They shared bedrooms but they loved that; they were close-knit, and they thrived on the feelings of warmth and belonging that come with being part of a big family. There was no loneliness at Jodey's; there was no shortage of playmates or team members for games.

In the summer, Karl and Jodey would take the children to the seaside or for day trips. Karl bought a minibus, so that they could all travel together. They were like local celebrities, all packed into the van, on an afternoon out for a pizza or to visit a funfair. Everyone knew Jodey as the 'Mother of Nine.' She was even approached by a national women's magazine who wanted to interview her about her brood. A writer came from London and Jodey loved sharing her story; she was so proud of her children. But when the article was published, and it was on sale around the neighbourhood, she started to have second thoughts.

"I'm not sure I like being the talk of the town," she frowned, flicking through the magazine.

Soon after, she and Karl were invited to take part in Channel 4's *Wife Swap*.

"Absolutely not," Jodey said. "I've had my five minutes of fame and I didn't like it. I'm quite happy as I am. No more photo shoots for me."

Life went on, and Jodey's days were taken up, packing school lunches, washing PE kits, mending leotards, scrubbing football boots and ironing uniforms. Each weekend, she'd cook a roast chicken dinner, or maybe mince and dumplings. Despite her disabilities, she was always brimming with enthusiasm and energy, forever making plans, organising treats and trips for the children. She took them out on long walks, and they often went swimming. Their house was on the edge of Stainsby Wood, a huge rural area of woodland. The kids spent hours playing in the woods, and one Christmas, they got quad bikes, so they could organise treks through the undergrowth. On rainy days, Jodey had endless patience with her children, inventing games with dolls and action figures, or baking playdough. One summer, she and Karl bought a tent and took the kids camping. But the weather was horrendous, and, after days of relentless rain, they admitted defeat and returned home, still soggy. The day after, predictably, the sun came out and Jodey had the brilliant idea of putting the tent up in their back garden instead. It was huge and brightly coloured, like a throw-back from Woodstock, and I laughed when I saw it sprawled over the entire garden.

Jodey threw in the sleeping bags and the toys, and the kids had picnics and sleepovers in there. They had a riot throughout the entire summer. "You have such a knack of knowing how to make those children happy," I told her. "I don't know how you do it." She smiled contentedly. Her recipe for success was quite simple, really. At heart, first and last, she was a true mother.

# 5
# Bitter Pills

Before the twins were even a year old, mid-way through 2001, Jodey's health hit a dramatic downward slide. Almost every morning, she was waking up in agony with her back. She was back and forth from her GP and each month seemed to bring a new hospital appointment, after which she would come home with yet another prescription and more physiotherapy exercises. One day, I visited, and she was slumped on the sofa, so drowsy that she was struggling to keep her eyes open.

"These new tablets are making me so sleepy," she complained. "I hate it. I can't look after the kids in this state."

We returned to the hospital, and she was offered different medication, but this time the tablets made her nauseous.

"These are no better," she said wearily. "I'm spending most of my day in the bathroom, waiting to throw up."

And meanwhile, the pain in her back was becoming worse and worse. Late in 2001, she was diagnosed with acquired kyphosis, a spinal condition. The following summer, after another spell in hospital, her doctors told her she had Klippel-Feil syndrome, a bone disorder distinguished by the abnormal fusion of bones in the neck. We were told the condition was very rare, and very painful. She was only 27 years old, so young, yet her body seemed to be failing her.

"Poor Jodey," I said, putting my arms around her. "It feels like you get all the rotten luck in the world."

"I feel like I'm falling to bits," she said miserably. "Every time I see a doctor, they find something else wrong with me."

And yet, it wasn't long before she was putting on a brave face and trying to carry on as normal, for the children's sake. Most days, she managed to dull the pain with a mixture of medication and determination. She could just about manage the school run, the washing and the shopping. But only just.

In February 2004, I was due to turn 50, a milestone birthday.

"We need to celebrate," Jodey insisted. "Let's have a party!"

I knew she wasn't really well enough to be organising a birthday bash, but I also knew she didn't want to let me down. She, Donna and Jamie all planned a party for me at my local social club, and, though I'd said I didn't want a fuss, we had a night to remember. It was lovely, being surrounded by all my family and friends. At the end of the evening, Jodey and I had our photo taken.

"Big smiles!" Jamie said, as he clicked away.

Afterwards, when I looked through the photos from the party, that picture struck a chord with me. For though Jodey was smiling, I could see the suffering, etched right across her face. It seemed now as though pain was a permanent part of her, an unwelcome guest in her body, long outstaying an unscheduled visit. That night, I went to bed, worrying about my daughter, all over again. I felt as though I'd come full circle, and I was right back in her teenage days, stressing about what lay ahead. I was all of a sudden very fearful of what the future held for her.

With her health still deteriorating, Jodey was referred that same year for more surgery, and she later had another operation on her back. But afterwards, she was so doped up with painkillers that she was virtually sedated. The months passed and she improved only slightly. Karl gradually took more and more responsibility at home. He did the food shopping, the cleaning and the washing, as well as holding down his job as a delivery driver. Slowly, he became the main carer for the children too. I was still popping round to the house every other day, to help out, but also to keep an eye on Jodey. And I was becoming more and more concerned. In addition to her physical ailments she was getting downhearted and depressed too. Her mental health was taking a real battering. All the signs were there, and I felt a pressure-cooker type tension, building in the house. It seemed as though things could not continue as they were. By now, she was on eight different types of medication; painkillers for her back, including morphine, as well as tablets to ease her psychological conditions. I was shocked, on one visit, to discover she was taking 23 tablets a day in total.

"Nefopam, Morphine Sulphate, Promethazine, Omeprazole, Pregabalin, MST Continus, Duloxetine, Amitriptyline... gosh Jodey," I paused for breath as I read down the list of her medication.

"If you shook me, I would rattle," she smiled, as she counted out her daily dose.

But I noticed the smile didn't reach her eyes. Not

anymore. There was a sadness about her; a sense of acceptance, as though she had already admitted defeat.

"This won't last," I urged. "You'll start to feel better soon, I promise."

She was taken into hospital yet again for an assessment of her back, and Karl was left somehow managing all on his own. I knew that for him, looking after Jodey was like having another, very needy, child. My heart went out to him too. He was doing all he could. But their marriage, like their family, was cracking and crumbling around them, and there was nothing anyone could do to stop it. The collapse seemed as inevitable as it was heart-breaking. For me, it felt like the end of a fairy-tale. And after Jodey came home from hospital this time, she barely left the house. She could no longer walk any real distance, and sometimes she would sleep solidly for a full day. Then, quite suddenly, in the middle of the night, numbed by painkillers, she would be seized by a burst of energy, and she might spend the early hours ironing and cleaning and cooking. More than once, she even went to the supermarket at midnight. Afterwards, exhausted, and crippled with pain, she would sleep for a further two days. It was manic behaviour, and typical of her psychological conditions. The problem with taking so many tablets was that they didn't all agree with each other, and so her behaviour, like her pain, was very erratic and hard to predict. Her lifestyle, like her sleep pattern, didn't really fit in with being a wife and a mother. She knew it as well as I did, but neither of us dared voice it out loud.

"You'll get back to normal soon," I kept saying, even though neither of us could really recall what normal was anymore.

One time, Jodey made a 3am trip to Asda, and came home with new cushions and some sale-price jewellery for the kids. They were hardly essential items, she knew that, and they certainly didn't merit going out in the dead of night whilst her family was asleep.

"I don't know what's wrong with me," she sighed, shrugging sadly. "They seemed like such a bargain at the time. I was really pleased with them."

Again, all I had to offer were platitudes and empty promises. We both knew this could not go on much longer. Early in 2009, I called round to find Jodey in bed, and sobbing into her pillow.

"Karl and me are splitting up," she wept. "We can't carry on like this. I'm moving out."

Deep down, I had known this was coming. But it was still somehow just as shocking and upsetting. Jodey was 34 years old, soon to turn 35, and she had been with Karl for more than half of her life. I knew that leaving him behind would hurt her terribly. But I also knew that leaving her children behind might well destroy her. For a woman who had defined herself through motherhood, who had built her entire life around her children, it was a catastrophic blow. Fatal, even. And yet I didn't blame Karl one bit. He was doing his best, looking after nine children and holding down a job too. And there was no way Jodey could look after the children on her own, on a long-term basis. She could hardly look after herself. This was nobody's fault. It was quite simply a cruel twist of fate.

"Come and stay with me," I offered.

But Jodey shook her head.

"I need to look after myself," she insisted.

I realised she was frightened of becoming totally reliant on other people and that she felt she had a point to prove in some way. She hadn't claimed benefits before, but now had to apply for Income Support. It was another small chip away at her independence. A few days later, Jamie called me to say Jodey was staying in a hostel. I threw my hands up in exasperation.

"Typical Jodey!" I sighed. "She is so difficult sometimes."

I knew better than to try to talk her round; Jodey had her way of doing things and interfering would only make it worse. And that stubborn streak had served her well in the past; it gave her a drive and a focus to overcome the challenges she faced. But I felt as though she was 15 years old again, marching out of the house with the social worker, throwing me a stroppy glare as she went. There was no way she would listen to me then – or now. Instead, I supported her where I could, going to the hostel each day and taking her shopping and home-made meals. I kept a look out for a new flat for her too. But then she announced that Eric had found her a place just over the road from Karl and the children.

"That sounds ideal," I said enthusiastically. "I'll help you move in."

\* \* \*

The flat was a new start and I wanted her to look forwards. But the location of the building was at once a blessing and a curse. Jodey wanted to be near the children, so that they could visit whenever they liked. It was near enough for them to sleep over or just to pop in to give her a cuddle without planning in advance. But each day, when she looked out of her flat, she saw her old home, she looked at the windows she had once cleaned, the flowerpots she had once planted, the front door which had once belonged to her. Living so near to her family was both a comfort and a torment. It was a constant reminder of what she had lost, and it was like pulling off a scab, over and over again.

"I'll get used to it, in time," she said.

I admired her confidence and resilience. And for a while, she seemed to manage quite well in the flat. But then, I noticed she was becoming very bloated, and she was struggling to stand up and walk properly. Her hands and feet puffed up quite alarmingly.

"Might be water retention," I said doubtfully. "Or an allergic reaction. You need to get checked out."

Jodey was taken into hospital, and as always seemed to be the way for her, it was far more serious than we had anticipated. Tests eventually showed she had an issue with her liver, caused by her long-term reliance on medication. Jodey wasn't a drinker at all; apart from the odd glass of wine at a party, or perhaps an occasional bottle of WKD, she didn't touch alcohol. Yet this made the diagnosis of liver problems seem even more cruel. It felt as though her bad luck was going on and on. Of course, now she needed more medication to counteract the effects of the previous medication. It was a circular hell, and she was trapped in it, with no way to escape.

My other two children had very few problems in comparison. Donna had two children of her own, she had studied History at university and was by now working as a teacher. Jamie had a daughter and ran his own successful carpet cleaning firm. But, of course, life wasn't about money or success. All I wanted – all any parent ever wants – is for their child to be happy and healthy. Jodey, tragically, was neither. Though Eric and I were no longer together, we had remained friends, and we communicated well regarding our worries over Jodey. He'd visit her one day, and me the other. Donna and Jamie called in regularly and the children popped in and out every day, showing her new trainers, grazed elbows or school merit awards. Jodey clung to the promise of those visits; those snippets of family life were her oxygen. And she longed desperately to be more involved and to be more of a mother.

"I love it when they're here, but the worst bit is the silence, after they've gone," she told me. "It's unbearable, being left here on my own. In some ways, the moment they're here, I'm dreading the moment they leave."

When the lease came up on the flat, we decided Jodey should come and stay with me for a while. For once she didn't object to me helping her, which I was pleased about, but I also knew it was a sign that she was relinquishing control. I hoped perhaps I could cheer her up, maybe catch up with her many hospital appointments, overhaul her medication, and help her to think more clearly and positively. I had only one bedroom in my flat, so I put a camp-bed in the living room, and it was a squash. But I loved having her back home with me.

"Just like the old days," she smiled.

For her supper, I toasted pikelets, the cheesy snacks she had loved as a kid. I filled hot water bottles to ease her back pain and made sure she did her physio programme. I picked out TV dramas and films for us to watch in the evenings. Jodey was a big fan of documentaries too. Then, the second series of *Benefits Street* was aired on Channel 4 and, to our amazement, it was filmed on the Tilery estate, where we had once lived when Jodey was a young teenager. We were glued to the telly, picking out people we recognised or streets that we knew.

"I've sunbathed on that park!" Jodey exclaimed. "Oh gosh, is that our old house, Mam? That one that's been converted into two flats?"

I popped my specs on and gave a hoot of surprise. Jodey was right. Our former home was now two flats and one of the main stars of the episode lived there.

"Let me see inside," I said, peering at the telly. "I wonder if they've changed that awful wallpaper. This is so exciting."

For a while, *Benefits Street* was our favourite programme. We were hooked, waiting eagerly for each weekly instalment and it was must-see TV for us. As a little girl, Jodey had loved films too, *Mary Poppins* was her favourite, and I managed to find a bargain copy on a DVD in a charity shop. In my own mind, I suppose I was trying to turn back time, right back to her childhood, and in doing so, to turn back her illness too. I would have given anything to press rewind on all of her pain. On my shopping trips, I picked up second-hand celebrity autobiographies, and we had hours of laughter reading out the most outrageous passages. Despite everything, Jodey had not lost her smile, or her sense of humour. She was still such good fun. But seeing her, all day, every day, was a reality check for me. In many ways, my daughter seemed much older than I was. She kept her medication in a weekly tablet organiser and would sometimes get mixed up with her dosage. More than once, we had to explain to the GP that she had used up her prescription early, by mistake.

"Sorry, it won't happen again," Jodey said, but the truth was her mind was so fuddled with all the medication she took, she couldn't always remember what she had taken.

Because of her back problems, her mobility was deteriorating; and she could manage to walk only short distances. She struggled even to make it round the supermarket or the short walk to the doctors' surgery. Emotionally, she was up and down too; she might be part way through a conversation and suddenly she would start to cry quietly. I was used to her mood swings, and the way she flipped helplessly between different aspects of her character. I was accustomed to her being very depressed one minute, to flying high the next. She had always struggled to regulate her emotions. Her sleep and eating patterns were unstable too and, again, that was nothing new. But I was beginning to see something different, this latest phase of her behaviour had an element of despair and resignation, and I was troubled by it. Late in 2015, Jodey was offered a new flat, on the third floor of a council high rise named Hume House in Stockton-on-Tees. She was excited to move in and Jamie, who had a car, generously ferried her belongings back and forth all day. Her older kids helped out too. Her new home was only a 10-minute bus ride away for me, or five minutes in a car.

"Shame I'm not on the top floor," Jodey said, as we unpacked clothes and pots and pans. "There's a brilliant view of the city, the higher you go."

The new flat was clean and light, and not too far from the shops. One of her friends had given her a pair of budgerigars, as a house-warming present, and the birds seemed to make the place more homely somehow. As much as she cursed the birds, I could see that Jodey was fond of them. That week, we found a second-hand sofa in the small ads and Jamie picked it up for her.

"It's so comfy," I said, as we both flopped down to test the cushions.

"I can really see myself curled up on this sofa watching telly," Jodey nodded. "I think I'm going to like living here."

Soon after she had settled in, Jodey rang to ask if I fancied a shopping trip.

"I'm feeling quite bright today," she told me. "I thought we should make the most of it."

She had a walking stick, and we went very slowly, but it was lovely to link my arm through hers, to see the sun on her face and to hear her laugh. As usual, she bought trinkets and little gifts for the kids; clothes, sweets, jewellery. By now, Jodey was a grandmother too and so she had all the more reason to enjoy spoiling her family. And still, she lived for their visits; seeing her children and their babies was what kept her going. Though her body was letting her down, in her mind, she was still very much a devoted mother. On Mother's Day 2016, Jodey handed me a bunch of flowers and a pink card with a teddy bear on the front. On the first page, she wrote:

'Your Buetifull.'

The spelling mistake made me smile and tear up all at once. It typified everything about Jodey and her problems; how she struggled to express herself and how she had been judged, through her life, by a lack of academic achievement and an inability to communicate and to conform. Yet I knew that she had a heart of gold, she had so much to offer, and many talents that 12 years of education had failed to unearth. On the second page of the card she had written:

'To the best mam in the world ever! I love you so so much. You are my inspiration, my everything, always.'

There was a pick and mix of lower case and capital letters and she had randomly underlined some of the verse. Again, that was Jodey all over; unpredictable, unique and so, so loveable. She had signed the message with 10 kisses; one from each of her nine children and one from her. I treasured the card, I had it on my mantelpiece for weeks, and later I popped it into my memory box for safe-keeping. I read and read those words, and it was so lovely to know that I was 'everything' to my daughter. But I could only hope and pray that I would be enough.

# 6
# Warning Signs

That summer of 2016, Jodey was admitted to hospital twice. The first time, she was treated for gastritis and duodenitis, and she was prescribed strong antibiotics before being sent home. Then, just weeks later, she picked up a severe chest infection, and needed another spell in hospital, and another course of antibiotics. I had to get two buses to the hospital, but I went to see her every day. Even as I approached the ward, I could hear Jodey's voice.

"Here, love, borrow mine, I won't use it, honestly."

When I got to her bedside, she was busy digging out her make-up mirror, to lend to another patient.

"Take my mascara as well," she offered. "A bit of slap makes you feel so much better."

Despite her own health issues, she was still thinking of other people; still putting them before herself. This time, she was in hospital for less than a week. But it seemed to me that one illness merged into the next; Jodey was so vulnerable, physically and mentally, that medically, she was something of a sitting duck. If there was any kind of bug going round, a cold or a stomach virus, she would always get it.

"The bugs must love me, that's all it is," she smiled.

At the end of summer 2016, her health spiralled even further. She would spend day after day stuck in bed and I often wasn't sure whether it was back pain or depression or a combination of the two that was keeping her there. I had a key to let myself into her flat and, one day, I found her sleeping in bed. I sat down softly next to her, on the duvet, and took her hand in mine. Her skin, against my own, felt so rough. And when I examined her fingers, they were dry, cracked and raw.

"You need a prescription for your skin, Jode," I said, when she awoke. "Your hands look so sore."

"Oh, my feet are just the same," she said, poking her toes out from under the covers.

"The doctor just said it's a side-effect of my medication. Another one! I don't think there's much I can do about it."

I brought her some new oily moisturiser. But it didn't help much, and the cracks in her skin added to her long list of woes. She'd had disability aids fitted in the flat; handrails at the front door and in the bathroom, and a seat in the shower, and she had a wheelchair too for long trips out. But really, it was of little use to her, because she lived alone on the third floor. She had to rely constantly on someone to visit to take her out, and I knew she hated that.

"What you really need is a mobility scooter," I decided. "We could store it downstairs in the foyer and it would give you back a bit of independence."

Jodey was by now receiving various benefits; Employment Support Allowance (ESA) Disability Living Allowance (DLA), as well as getting some relief with her rent and council tax. I wrote to the DWP, to ask if she could have a mobility scooter too. For me, it made perfect sense because a scooter would improve Jodey's physical and mental health. But inexplicably, the request was turned down.

"Honestly, don't these people care?" I said crossly.

I wasn't about to give up, however. I even looked into buying Jodey a scooter myself, but the cheapest were more than £1,000 and I didn't have that kind of money. I then applied for a loan, but my application was refused.

"I'll save up," I promised her. "I'll put a bit by each week. You'll see. By the time the weather improves, I'll have enough, and you can go out in the sunshine."

Each day, after I'd finished my own housework, I'd get the bus to see Jodey. Quite often, as I was standing at the bus-stop, I'd get a text:

'You on the bus yet, Mam? Can't wait to see you!'

If Jamie wasn't working, he'd give me a lift, and the journey took just a matter of minutes. Sometimes, I went to the chemist on my way there, to collect Jodey's long list of prescriptions. Other times, I called at the supermarket and brought her some shopping. Or I might cook for her at home and carry a warm casserole, wrapped in a tea towel, on my knees on the bus. I let myself in with my key, and if she was asleep, I kept busy cleaning or doing a bit of ironing. One morning she called to say her electricity was on the blink and so I hurried down to the bus stop to help her sort it out.

"I'm on my way," I texted. "Sit tight, pet."

Another time, she messaged to say she was freezing cold, and I rummaged through my spare room to find an electric heater I rarely used. Then, I asked Jamie to drive it over there for her.

"Warmth is on the way!" I messaged her. "Look out for your brother out of the window."

Yet another day, she rang in a panic:

"Mam! There's a wasps' nest outside the window! Can you come and look at it for me?"

I laughed. I was not a pest-control expert, but I took a detour to the shops to pick up a can of wasp spray, and I hopped on the bus.

"Extermination expected imminently!" I texted.

Slowly – and it wasn't lost on me – Jodey was becoming more and more like a little girl again. She called me with the slightest little problem, which of course I welcomed, because I wanted to support her. But seeing her regress so sharply broke my heart too. The cruelty of her illness was not primarily the pain. It was that it ate away at who Jodey was; a mother, a daughter, a woman who loved her family and who loved life. Slowly, chip by chip, her personality was being eroded.

For a treat, she loved a packet of brightly coloured rainbow drop sweets and an energy drink. She liked the same sort of snacks as the kids and she would always eat all her sweets at once, ignoring my suggestions that she should make them last. Even if I bought her five bags, she'd polish off the lot that same day.

"You'll make yourself sick, Jode," I said in concern.

I wondered whether her medication was making her even more impulsive, more juvenile almost. Like a teenager, she lived very much in the now. It was another, heart-wrenching sign that she was rewinding back to childhood and that her character was crumbling, bit by bit. Occasionally, I'd call in at the chippy and buy fish, chips and mushy peas for us both. They were an old favourite of hers. Standing in the takeaway queue, I often thought back to Jodey, in her wedding dress, with a bag of chips in her hands. Her wedding had been such a lovely day and I'd felt as though she had the world at her feet. Often, I'd turn up at her door with the chips as a surprise, and her face always lit up when I turned the corner into her living room.

"I could smell those when you were walking down the corridor," she'd say with a big grin.

They were happy, comfortable times, both of us balancing a tray on our knees on her two-seater couch, flicking through the TV guide, the smell of vinegar stinging our eyes.

"Mam! You've more chips than me! I've counted!"

"I'll swap you a spoonful of peas. Deal or no deal?!"

Later, at the bus-stop, I might be shivering in the rain, or inwardly grumbling about the bus running late, and my phone would flash with a message.

"Thanks for today, Mam. I appreciate it. I love you so much."

I would have stood there all night in the pouring rain, just to get a message like that. The love of my daughter made everything worthwhile.

\* \* \*

Most weeks, Jodey had an appointment with her local doctor or at the hospital. Her GP would make a home visit if Jodey wasn't up to leaving the flat but often, I'd persuade her to make the short trip to the surgery, as an excuse for her to get some fresh air.

"It's not good for you to be cooped up in your flat seven days a week," I said.

With the GP, Jodey was sometimes in trouble for taking too much of her medication at once.

"I get muddled up," she complained. "And anyway, sometimes the pain is so bad, I just have to take another tablet. It's the only way to get some peace."

The GP was always patient with her, but he was worried about the consequences of too much medication for her. And sometimes it seemed to me that the side-effects of certain drugs were worse than the symptoms they were supposed to cure. We were going round and round in circles.

"I'll keep a closer eye on her," I promised the doctor.

Jodey was also under the care of a consultant psychiatrist at The James Cook University Hospital in Middlesbrough and an orthopaedic specialist at The University Hospital of North Tees. I went with her to each appointment. We'd make a day of it and get a coffee and a crumpet in a café on our way home. If Jodey was up to it, we'd do a quick trawl of the pound shops too for some bargains. Still, despite every step causing her pain, she loved to shop.

Jodey never slept well; partly because of the pain and also because some of her medication prevented her from sleeping soundly too. Often, at 3am, my phone would bleep, and I'd wake to a message from Jodey.

"Can't sleep, Mam," she wrote. "Are you awake?"

"I am now!" I replied, laughing. "I'll get my dressing gown and make a brew."

"I will as well. You having tea or hot chocolate?"

Often, we'd chat or message for ages during those lonely hours when the rest of the world was asleep. I'd curl up in my armchair with my phone on my knee, waiting for the next beep.

"Sorry for waking you up," she'd say. "Just I get so scared on my own."

But I always waved her apologies aside. I wanted her to wake me – I wanted her to rely on me. She needed me now more than ever before. Sometimes, in the darkness, as I typed out messages of reassurance, I was transported right back to when Jodey was a baby, screaming in the cot, her little face red and furious as she demanded to be picked up and cuddled. For hours, at night, it was just me and her. And it was the same now. She was no longer so angry, thank goodness. But still, she needed that human contact. Still, she needed to feel loved.

There were spells when Jodey barely slept at all, and her mental health became very shaky. She could no longer think straight when she was so exhausted, and she could whip herself up into a panic over something very trivial. Luckily, I could call on the crisis team if I felt she was spiralling, and several times, Jodey was admitted to a psychiatric unit for short stays. It was only ever for a few nights. But she never felt the intervention did her much good.

"I'm better off here, in my own place," she said.

In the autumn of 2016, Jodey began complaining of a new pain all around her body, and particularly behind her eyes and her ears.

"I'll make you an appointment with the doctor," I said to her. "Perhaps it's connected with your medication."

But I could tell she wasn't coping too well. She looked pale and tired, and she was more out of breath even than usual. Even on her off-days, Jodey had always been glamorous, and she made an effort with her make-up and clothes. She liked to dye her hair, light brown or blonde, and occasionally she'd have streaks put in for her birthday or Christmas. And when she could no longer shop for her own fashions, she followed the trends vicariously through her daughters. She loved costume jewellery, rings especially, and we liked to joke she had a handbag addiction. Her handbags hung over the door of her wardrobe, all bright splashes of colour, cruelly reminiscent of the carefree girl she had once been.

"You've a handbag for every day of the week," I smiled.

But I noticed now that she was making less and less effort with her appearance. She didn't seem to have the energy anymore and, of course, she rarely left her home so there was little point in her dressing up. The handbags gathered dust and her collection of shoes and boots sat on the rack by the door, forgotten and forlorn. I wondered whether she'd ever get back to her old self again.

\* \* \*

With Christmas on the horizon, I thought it might be a good excuse to cheer Jodey up with a shopping trip.

"If you're up to it, we could go into town, get some early bargains," I suggested.

She didn't seem too keen at first, I knew she was worried about the pay-back, because a day at the shops was, for her, inevitably followed by a day of unbearable pain. But I also knew how much she loved a spot of Christmas shopping, and how she liked to get started early with her lists and her wrapping.

"Have a think about it," I said to her. "We could have a look at the Christmas lights too."

One morning soon after, I let myself in with my key as usual, and to my surprise Jodey was sitting on the sofa, dressed and with her coat buttoned up.

"Come on, let's hit the shops," she said, with her best effort at enthusiasm.

"Smashing," I beamed.

It took us some time just to get into the lift and then out into the fresh air, but Jodey smiled when the cold air pinched her skin. She had her walking stick and took regular rests to get her breath back. It was my job to find the next bench or the next wall where we could sit.

"Here we are, sit yourself down and relax," I said.

But in spite of the frequent stops, we had a lovely day. Jodey's problems were always there but the sparkle of Christmas outshone the shadow of her illness and we trawled from shop to shop, filling bag after bag. We hadn't much money of course, Jodey's benefits didn't stretch to luxuries really, but between us we had years of experience in smelling out the best bargains.

"We're a good team, Mam," Jodey laughed, as I pounced on a pile of two-for-one Christmas socks.

Jodey bought a pair for all the younger kids, and I even got a pair for myself. Jodey grinned as I popped mine into the basket.

"You're never too old for a pair of Christmas socks," I reminded her.

She laughed again and I saw the colour flood through her pale cheeks.

"I think shopping is by far the best medicine for you," I smiled. "It has really done you good today."

Jodey bought calendars and clothes for the children, along with toys and nick-nacks for her grandchildren. By now, her eldest was 25 and her youngest, the second set of twins, were 16. She had six gorgeous little grandchildren too. Towards the end of the afternoon, I steered Jodey into a café for a cup of tea.

"My treat," I said. "You look like you need a proper sit down."

Jodey sank gratefully into a chair and propped her walking stick up at the side. I queued for tea and a cake to share. Jodey seemed uncharacteristically serious as she took a sip of her drink, and then she looked me straight in the eye and said:

"If anything happens to me, Mam, don't go screaming,"

I stared back, and a chill ran right through me. Despite the warmth of my drink, I felt as though I had icy water rushing through my veins.

"What do you mean?" I stuttered. "Where has this come from, Jode? What's wrong?"

But Jodey didn't reply. She continued to sip her tea, and to look straight ahead, and so I tried to change the subject and throw off my anxiety. We'd had a great time and I didn't want the day to be spoiled. Yet all the way home, the worry was there. It was such an odd thing to say, and even in bed that night, it gnawed away at the inside of my brain, like a rodent. I decided, as I replayed the phrase in my head, that it was probably no more than an irrational outburst, that she was probably worried about her health, and especially about the new pains in her head, her eyes and ears. She was no doubt dwelling too much on her own mortality, I told myself, and I vowed to forget it and move on. Even so, the words stuck with me, like a pebble, jamming my throat.

\* \* \*

After our early Christmas shopping trip, Jodey's breathing became even more laboured. One night, at 3am, my phone bleeped with a text.

"Mam, I can barely get my breath," she wrote. "I can't lie down without coughing."

"This isn't fair on you," I replied. "I'll sort it out as soon as the surgery opens."

At 8am, I booked her an emergency appointment with the doctor. And when the GP came out, he listened to her chest and shook his head.

"Sounds to me like you have pneumonia," he said. "And a touch of pleurisy too. We need to get you into hospital."

In a way, I was relieved. I hated the idea of Jodey gasping for breath, on her own, each night. At least in hospital she would be well looked after. There were many times I'd asked her if she wanted to come and stay with me overnight, just for company, but it was a big effort for her to sleep somewhere else, and of course my place didn't have the disability aids that she relied on. Besides, I was wary of stamping out those last little scraps of independence and confidence; I was worried she couldn't cope alone, but I didn't want her to know that. She needed to think that I had every faith in her, despite my misgivings.

"It's probably only for a few days," I consoled, as I packed a bag of pyjamas and toiletries. "And I'll be there every day, never fear."

She went into hospital by ambulance and later that afternoon, I made sure I was there to speak to the doctor for her.

"She's been having pain behind her eyes and her ears," I said. "Could that be connected to the pneumonia in some way?"

"We'll do a scan," the consultant promised.

The following morning, he came to see us at Jodey's bedside with the results. He took a deep breath, and said:

"I'm sorry, Jodey, we've found a pincal cyst on your brain. That might explain some of the facial pain you've been having recently. This issue is in addition to the pneumonia."

My heart sank. This was yet more bad news; more trauma, heaped upon my daughter.

"Is it serious?" I stuttered. "Can you operate?"

The doctor explained the cyst was benign and currently measured 9mm. At 10mm they would consider taking action and possibly operate, if Jodey's symptoms continued. Her eyes widened a little as she listened to the doctor's words. She didn't cry and she showed very little emotion, but by now, she was practically numb to health dramas. She was so used to her body letting her down that one more problem, even though it was a cyst in her brain, hardly registered with her.

"We'll do another scan in a few months, as an outpatient," the doctor decided. "For now, we need to focus on the pneumonia."

Two weeks on, Jodey was discharged from hospital, just in time for the run-up to Christmas. I helped decorate her little flat with a small artificial Christmas tree, another of my bargain buys, and a string of lights.

"There," I said, standing back. "What do you think?"

Jodey smiled but even to me the display looked somehow lonely and pitiful this year, especially when I thought back to the extravagant and fun-filled family Christmases she had organised in the past. Christmas, like everything else, was scaled down. I felt as though the celebrations were petering out, slowly, year by year. But then I snuffed out the thought quickly. This was no time to be negative. Donna had invited us all to her house for Christmas dinner, but Jodey had decided to go to her eldest daughter, Louise, for Christmas Day. On Christmas Eve, I arrived at the flat, with my arms piled high with presents; perfume, a fancy diary, and some cash in a card. Jodey had bought me a pair of fluffy slippers and a heart shaped soap with my name on it.

"The soap is far too pretty to use," I smiled.

Jodey was hoping to see her children on Boxing Day, and so that afternoon, I went out and bought bags of party food in anticipation. I knew how inadequate and insignificant Jodey felt at Christmas more than any other time. Her whole life had once been all about her children and in years gone by, she would have been the one out shopping and then wrapping, cleaning and cooking. Now, she was the one on the sidelines. She was a mother in name only. Instead of looking after others, we were looking after her. She was reliant on us all and it was very sad to see. The next morning, I phoned her early.

"Happy Christmas!" I said, more cheerfully, in truth, than I felt.

"Same to you, Mam," Jodey replied, and I got the impression that she, too, was putting on a brave face.

Neither of us wanted to spoil the other's day. In the afternoon, I called her again, but she was already back home.

"I got Louise to bring me back. I'm just not up to it," she said. "I'm going to go to bed."

Not wanting to spoil the festivities for the family, I stayed at Donna's, pulled crackers, played party games and helped with the washing up. But all afternoon, my thoughts were clouded with concern. It really wasn't like Jodey to give up on Christmas, especially when she had been so excited to spend time with her children.

"Sure you're all right, love?" I asked when I called in the next day.

"I'm OK, Mam," she replied. "Don't be worrying. I just get tired, that's all."

I had never made a special fuss on New Year's Eve and often I was in bed before midnight even struck. But this year, I felt, inexplicably, that I wanted to be with Jodey. We saw the New Year in together, in our slippers, nursing a hot chocolate each.

"Let's hope this New Year brings some good news," I said, giving her a hug.

But again, I had the impression that I was going through the motions, saying what was expected of me and not what I really believed. Even to me, my words sounded hollow and unconvincing. In the pit of my stomach, I had a knot of anxiety, a sense of doom, that I just couldn't shake.

That week, I slipped into church and said a silent prayer for my daughter.

"Look after her, please," I pleaded.

January was a hard month for everyone with the return to work and to normality, and often a depressing time too. And so, I was especially worried about Jodey. I knew she was prone to troughs of emotion and that she would be particularly fragile right now. I saw her every day, sometimes twice a day. The weather was drizzly and damp and it was often hard going, waiting at the bus stop. But all I needed was just one text from Jodey –

'Thanks Mam. Loved seeing you today!'

And it was enough to brighten up the gloomiest weather. Mostly, she'd be in bed when I arrived, and I had the usual nagging concerns that she wasn't eating properly or looking after herself. After the pneumonia, she was easily exhausted and needed more rest, yet still she battled against insomnia. By now, she was seeing her GP fortnightly, and mid-way through January, I made another appointment because her back was giving her a lot of pain. She was referred for another course of physiotherapy and the GP warned her, once again, about taking too many painkillers.

"I don't do it on purpose," Jodey replied. "Sometimes I get mixed up, I forget whether or not I've taken my tablets. Other times, I'm in so much pain that I can't stand it."

I knew the medication was harmful long-term. But I also knew that Jodey was finding it really difficult to think long-term at all. The thought sent a shiver right through me and I blocked it out.

# 7

# Penniless

On January 17, I visited her as usual, and in the foyer of the flats, I collected her post from her pigeonhole. Amongst all the junk mail and flyers, I spotted an official-looking letter in a brown envelope.

"Look at this, pet," I said as I handed over the pile of mail. "DWP stamp on the front. Might be important."

Jodey ripped it open and began reading. And her face darkened as she followed the words.

"The DWP say they might stop my benefits," she said, her voice wavering. "I missed an appointment with them, or something. I don't know what they're talking about."

"What?" I replied, shaking my head. "Don't be daft, they can't do that. Let me read it."

I took the letter from her hands, feeling sure she had made a mistake. But the contents didn't really make much sense to me either. The DWP was suggesting that Jodey had failed to attend an earlier workability capability assessment (WCA) and, as a result, her benefits might be stopped.

"What assessment?" I asked. "What appointment?"

Jodey shrugged.

"First I've heard of it," she said. "I'd never ignore anything from the DWP, you know that. I rely on my benefits too much."

"Well, this can't be right," I replied briskly. "Let's phone them now and get it sorted out."

According to the letter, Jodey had been booked in for an assessment the previous day, January 16. The DWP claimed she'd had an earlier letter in December, to notify her about it.

"I didn't get a letter from them in December," Jodey frowned. "I've had no calls, no visits, nothing."

Her postbox was in the foyer of the flats, three floors down, and so Jodey didn't always get her post on the day it was delivered, because she often wasn't well enough to get out of bed, never mind make her way down three floors. Often, I'd check it for her whilst I was visiting.

"But I don't remember seeing a DWP letter either," I pondered.

But in any case, she certainly wasn't well enough to attend any kind of assessment. She had been in hospital, of course, with pneumonia, and since then had been too ill much of the time to even get dressed each day. I dialled the DWP helpline and handed the phone to Jodey. She was on hold for what seemed like an age before she was finally connected to a human voice. But he simply advised her to fill in the form which had come in the envelope along with the letter. She was told that was her only way of communicating with them. Jodey hung up, her face bleached white with worry.

"What a waste of time," I said crossly. "We've been on the phone for ages and all for nothing."

Together, we filled in the form, explaining that Jodey had been in hospital with pneumonia and a cyst on the brain, and that she'd never received any invitation to an assessment. We also pointed out that, in any case, Jodey was disabled and housebound and would need a home assessment. She included details for her GP and asked the DWP to contact the surgery to verify everything she had said.

"That will sort it," I said confidently, as I popped the form in an envelope. "Don't worry about it, Jode. It's just a mix-up."

We also wrote a letter directly to the GP, asking him to contact the DWP himself. I posted the forms on my way home that same afternoon, feeling that we had ticked every box. Really, I wasn't too concerned, and I felt certain that someone at the DWP had made an error which could be resolved quite easily with some common sense. Like anyone else, I was rightly outraged by the minority who claimed benefits they didn't need and weren't entitled to. I was all for digging out those liars and cheats who abused the system. But my Jodey was someone who absolutely needed every penny of her benefits. She couldn't survive without them. If anything, I believed she was probably in need of more help, not less, because her health was deteriorating so rapidly. And so I was sure the mistake would be cleared up quickly. Each day, I checked her pigeonhole, waiting for a reply.

"Anything, Mam?" she'd ask, as I let myself into the flat.

"Sorry pet, not today. Maybe tomorrow."

As the days passed, the stress ate away at her, and she became increasingly jittery and tearful. I knew she was slowly working herself up into a frenzy, and I also knew there was little she or anyone else could do to stop it.

\* \* \*

On January 23, I was so worried about Jodey that I called the GP for an emergency appointment. She seemed to be in such a state. She was unable to sit still for a moment, even to have a glass of water and a painkiller.

"Come on," I cajoled her. "Have a drink and let's put the telly on."

But she was very agitated, jumping from one thought to the next, with very little sense or coherence. The GP came out and agreed that Jodey was suffering from stress and also found that she had a throat infection.

"She's having some problems with her benefit payments," I explained. "It's too much for her to cope with."

On February 6, the DWP letter finally arrived. Picking it up from the pigeonhole, I recognised the same style of brown envelope as before. Yet if it had been dropped from the sky by a great black vulture, I could not have felt a greater sense of foreboding. I hurried up the stairs and down the corridor, clutching it in my hand. Jodey quickly scanned the letter and her face crumpled.

"I can't believe this," she said, in a whisper. "Why are they doing this to me? Mam, why?"

Over her shoulder, I read, with complete incredulity, that the DWP had decided there was no good reason for Jodey not to have attended the assessment appointment.

"No good reason!" I spluttered. "Except that you didn't even know about it! Except that you've been in hospital with pneumonia and a cyst on the brain! You take 23 tablets a day and you can hardly walk! Is that not good enough?"

It wasn't like me to lose my temper, but my blood was boiling. The letter was farcical. And deeply offensive.

It was as if it had been written about someone else entirely. With shaking hands, I dialled the job centre.

"You need to fill in a form," said a bored voice on the other end of the line. "We'll send you one out."

Drawing in my breath to stay calm, I tried once again to explain how desperate we were, how upset and ill Jodey was, but it was useless. Wearily, I agreed to fill in the form, because I knew there was no point getting into an argument. As I hung up the phone, I wished that the person on the other end could have seen Jodey, slumped on the sofa, her entire body trembling, her eyes shiny with tears. She already had so much to cope with. Why would anyone treat her like this?

"What will I do if they stop my money, Mam?" she mumbled anxiously. "What will I do?"

"It won't come to that," I said gently. "Nobody would be that cruel."

But I no longer felt so sure of myself. The very next day, February 7, 2017, I picked up a dreaded brown envelope from the postbox in the foyer and carried it upstairs. Jodey was propped up in bed, so I perched on the side of her duvet and opened it for her.

"Oh no," I gasped. "Love, I'm so sorry. They've stopped your benefits."

The letter said that Jodey would receive no further payments of ELA, DLA, housing benefit or council tax benefit. She flopped back on her pillows as if the air had been squeezed from her. We both stared, wordless and shell-shocked, at the page. The typing fuzzed and blurred before my eyes as I read and re-read the text, convinced that somehow, I must have misunderstood. But no, the meaning was there, clear and cruel, and quite astonishingly offering no support and no alternative means of income. I had the sensation of being punched hard in the stomach and each breath was desperately painful. I had no idea how Jodey was going to manage without any money at all. This was supposed to be a caring society, Britain was a first-world country, a land of affluence and prosperity. Yet this was also a place where disabled people were cut off without a penny. I remembered a passage from *A Christmas Carol*; it was one of Donna's favourite books and we'd read it together many times when she was at school.

'Are there no workhouses? ...If they would rather die they had better do it and decrease the surplus population.'

Scrooge's words cut deep, as I read the letter yet again. Dickens was writing in 1843. Yet in 2017, very little seemed to have changed for people like Jodey. I remembered, too, our time living on the Tilery estate, now infamous as 'Benefits Street'. What a mockery that Jodey, a former resident, had been stripped of her own benefits and with that her only means of survival, without so much as a home visit or even a phone call from anyone at the DWP. To say they didn't care about her one bit was an understatement.

I read the letter one last time and sighed heavily. Next to me, I caught sight of Jodey's ashen face, and I could see the panic scudding through her eyes, like rain clouds. I took her hand in mine and did my best to look confident and business-like.

"We'll fight this," I said firmly, digging a pen out of my handbag. "Let's appeal. Right now."

But Jodey just stared at me, blankly. It struck me that I was angrier than she was. She seemed somehow already overcome, as though her battle was lost before it had even begun. And that just made me feel even more angry, on her behalf; that she was expected to humiliate and degrade herself in order to have her voice heard. Why pick on those who were least able to fight back and defend themselves? It was so wrong. So wrong.

That same morning, I posted the appeal back to the DWP. The next day, and the next, we heard nothing back from them. My nerves jangled each time I unlocked the postbox in the foyer. I was so desperate for their reply and yet at the same time terrified of it arriving. I longed for it, I dreaded it, I even dreamed about it. That letter dominated my mind, awake and asleep. But each day, I had to face Jodey with the same response.

"Nothing,"

"Nothing."

"Nothing again. Sorry, love."

On February 13, I celebrated my 63rd birthday. I bought a little sponge cake myself and took it round to Jodey's. I knew the shame of not being able to afford to buy me a cake would wound her deeply, even though a party was the last thing on my mind. When I arrived, she presented me with a card and flowers.

"I asked Louise to get them for me," she said apologetically. "I'm sorry, Mam. I wanted to get you a proper present, but I couldn't afford it."

"Forget all about my birthday," I told her. "Let's get your benefits sorted out, and we can celebrate at a later date."

Late that morning, some of Jodey's children arrived, and it was a squash, but a pleasant one, in the tiny flat.

I knew Jodey loved occasions like these with her family around her.

"Tell you what, let's all go outside for a photo," I suggested.

But to my surprise, Jodey shook her head.

"I can't make it outside," she stuttered. "I'm not well enough. Not today."

"Never mind," I said. "Let's have a photo of me and you here, on the sofa, instead."

But again, Jodey shook her head.

"Sorry, I'm not up to it," she replied flatly. "Look at my hair. I've no make-up on. I just don't feel like it."

Though I tried not to show it, I was very taken aback. Jodey usually loved having her photo snapped. Once, years earlier, she'd had a professional photo shoot done for her birthday. In days gone by, she had always been glamorous and fashionable and was the first one in front of the camera. But not today. She could hardly make eye contact with me. It was a warning flag, flapping on the horizon, just inside my line of vision, but coming ever closer.

"Don't worry," I said lightly. "It's no big deal."

After cake and coffee, everyone went home. And that afternoon, still with nothing from the postman, Jodey began worrying that her appeal letter had perhaps been mislaid.

"I'll do another letter," I promised. "Can't do any harm."

Together, we drafted another letter, begging the DWP to reconsider. I went out to post it immediately.

"That should do the trick," I said, with a confidence I didn't feel.

The following day, Jodey's postbox was full, but this time with letters from the council tax department and from her housing association landlord, asking for payment. They had not received her relief payments because the DWP had cancelled them.

"I don't have the money," she said bluntly. "What can I do?"

Jodey received ESA and DLA each week, totalling just over £120, along with the allowances for rent and council tax. After paying her bills for utilities and food, she had barely enough to live on. On a good week, after her bills were paid, she might have enough left for a few cheap treats, and they were usually for her children. I kept half an eye on her finances to make sure she was coping, but I did not pry too much, because I didn't want her to think that I was taking over. It was another way of me trying to encourage her independence. But I was certain of one thing. Jodey had no savings, no rainy day account, no back-up plan. Without her benefits, she was penniless. She was drowning.

"Mam, what will I do?" she asked again. "What's going to happen to me?"

My heart felt ripped into two as I watched her, shrinking into the sofa, recoiling, like an injured animal. Her hands were cracked and weeping with sores and her whole body trembled with anxiety. The pain seemed to ooze from every pore of her body. I wondered how anyone could ever come to the decision that she did not deserve help.

'What has happened to compassion?' I wanted to scream. "What has happened to our society, if we cannot look after our sick and our disabled?'

In that moment it seemed to me as though all hope was lost; not just for Jodey and me, but for all of us. I felt nothing but disgust for a world that would treat its vulnerable with such disdain and contempt. I wanted to wail at the top of my voice at the sheer cruelty and injustice. But I did none of that. It was my job, as a mother, to stay strong and resilient for Jodey. Instead, I rooted in my purse and pulled out a £20 note.

"Here, pet," I said, pushing it into her hand.

Jodey shook her head miserably. I was a pensioner by now, retired, and scrabbling around for money myself. Jodey knew I really couldn't afford to help her out. But I insisted.

"Take it," I said. "You can pay me back when we get your benefits rolling again."

Even so, the look of shame in her eyes, as she murmured her thanks, sent a chill down my spine. As much as she worried about having no money, it pained her even more to accept it from me.

"That's what mams are for," I told her.

That night, I went through my kitchen cupboards and packed tins of soup and tuna and baked beans. My bag was heavy and clunked noisily on the bus the following morning. From the stop, I puffed and panted my way up to Jodey's front door, with aching shoulders and a heavy heart. I couldn't believe it had come to this.

"This should keep you going," I said, as I stacked the tins in her cupboard.

I opened a can of tomato soup for dinner, and we shared it, without bread. Jodey had no tea bags left, so I couldn't even make us a brew. I felt wretched.

"I'll nip to the shops after my soup," I said. "Pick a few things up for you, Jode."

"I'm going back to bed," Jodey replied. "Sorry Mam, I'm so cold, and I can't afford to have the heating on."

Her flat was chilly, I'd noticed it too. I'd kept my coat on whilst we ate. As I washed our two bowls and spoons, I was hit with yet another wave of shock and repulsion. How could we call ourselves a civilised society?

"Please sir, can I have some more?' I said to myself, holding up an empty bowl from the soapsuds.

"We might as well be back in Victorian times!"

After I'd tidied up, I went to check on Jodey in the bedroom. She had the quilt pulled up to her chin, and she was wearing woolly gloves too.

"So, you're not thinking of sunbathing any time soon, then?" I joked, raising my eyebrows.

It was only a light-hearted comment, a feeble attempt to cheer her up. But Jodey just stared ahead, her eyes fixed, and she said nothing. I couldn't remember the last time I'd seen her smile; really smile.

"Come on, Jode," I said softly.

In the past, we'd always been able to see the humour in things, to have a gossip and a giggle about everyday problems. Jodey's favourite programme was *Call The Midwife* and we loved watching it together at weekends and then picking over the plot lines. We were both big soap fans too and Jodey especially liked the reality TV shows about glamorous housewives. When she was well, she liked picking up fashion tips from those programmes and then searching out cheaper replicas on the high street. She was a sucker for bling. And no matter how desperate her physical and mental health had been, over the years, she had always retained her zest for life and her sense of fun. But today, she was drained of enthusiasm and energy. She seemed devoid of thought and of conversation. She could only nod, mutely, in reply to my efforts to engage her about Cain Dingle and Steve McDonald, and in the end, I abandoned my small talk and climbed onto the bed to give her a cuddle instead.

"Come on, love," I said again. "We'll get through this, you and me."

Jodey didn't speak, but I could feel her shoulders shaking, as she wept, and my own tears flowed freely too.

"We'll get through it," I murmured again, and though I was whispering, the desperation in my voice rang out in the cold air.

* * *

The next day, February 15, there was, incredibly, still no response from the DWP about Jodey's appeal.

"What could be more urgent than this appeal?" I tutted, as I shut the postbox again. "Why are they taking so long when they know she has no money?"

I had previously made an appointment with the Citizens Advice service and, later that day, I insisted that Jodey got dressed. Together, we got wrapped up, ready to leave her flat.

"The fresh air will do you good," I encouraged her. "Make sure you take your hat and gloves."

Jodey wasn't well enough to be out, I was painfully aware of that. But neither was she well enough to withstand the intolerable strain of having no money. Before we left, I bundled up all the letters I could find in various drawers and took them with us. It was such a challenge for Jodey to make the short trip from her flat to the Citizens Advice offices, and we had to stop several times for her to get her breath. Luckily, I spotted a bench, and we had a few moments there to let her rest.

When we arrived at the offices, we were ushered straight in and Jodey was offered a chair and a glass of water.

"Can you help us?" I pleaded, whilst Jodey took a few moments to settle. "My daughter is at her wits' end. The DWP has left her high and dry."

The assistant, Susan, was shocked when she heard what Jodey was going through.

"Absolutely, we will try to help you," she said.

Just to hear those words, to know that someone was on our side, was such a comfort. Susan began reading through the bundle of letters and notes I had brought so that she could familiarise herself with Jodey's situation. Amongst all the junk, she found a letter, still in a sealed envelope and quite clearly unopened.

"May I?" she asked, and Jodey nodded.

It was a letter dated December 15, from the DWP, inviting Jodey for a Work Capability Assessment.

"This is the letter!" I exclaimed as Susan began to read the contents out loud. "This is the letter! Jodey has never even read it, she has never even opened it, and yet they have stopped her benefits!"

This was proof, tangible and incontrovertible proof, that Jodey had never known about the invite to the WCA.

"Surely, now, she will get her benefits back?" I asked.

"We will do our best," Susan promised me.

There and then, she wrote to the DWP herself, explaining Jodey's predicament in detail. As we stood up to leave, she also handed us a voucher for the local food bank.

"It's not much but it might help," she said, taking Jodey's hands in hers.

Since Jodey's benefits had been stopped, Susan was the first person to treat her like a human being and to take her seriously. I would never be able to express what her kindness meant to me.

"I can't thank you enough," I said, as we walked out into the cold.

\* \* \*

The next day, though there was no letter from the DWP, Jodey received a utilities bill for £45.00, which, of course, she had no way of paying. She handed the bill to me silently, her eyes downcast.

"Look, I can borrow the money, we'll find a way to pay it," I said. "Don't think about the bills, not today."

But we both knew that wasn't the answer. The bills, like the problems, were piling up on top of Jodey and soon she would be buried underneath them. We could not borrow money for every bill, and neither could I afford to bail her out. And the money was not even the main issue; the humiliation and the shame of relying on other people for everything was corrosive. Jodey's dignity was being stripped away, day by day, slice by slice.

That afternoon, I left Jodey huddled in bed, and I went out to the food bank to use the voucher which Susan had given to us. I was handed a small bag of essentials; bread, rice, a few tins. There was even a small packet of biscuits.

"Thank you," I beamed. "She will be over the moon."

It wasn't much, just one carrier bag full, but I was bowled over with gratitude. To me, the food bank volunteers were like angels – angels in cheap overalls, in a draughty building, in a rotten world. But angels all the same.

"I don't know what we'd do without you," I added. "Really, you're saving lives doing this. I hope you know that."

I bit back my tears, determined not to let myself cry. But the lady on the door gave me a quick hug as I was leaving, and that small gesture of solidarity was enough to break my resolve. The tears poured down my cheeks as I walked back to Jodey's. These past few weeks, I had hardened myself against giving in to emotion; I'd had to, to stay strong for Jodey. But this one small kindness had touched me in a way that the corporate cruelty of the DWP never could. That lady – whose name I would never even know – was a small glimmer of hope; a pinprick of light on my very dark landscape. She was my life-raft and my reminder that humanity still existed.

"Thank you," I murmured as I made my way along the pavements. "Thank you."

She was far behind me now, but I prayed that she would hear my voice.

The following morning, I made the now familiar check in Jodey's little postbox to look for her mail. Again, it was empty. Was this some sort of sick joke? It was a mistake to invite her to an assessment she didn't know about and was not well enough to attend. It was unforgivable to then cut off her benefits. And it was a further twist of the knife for her appeal to now be ignored.

Everything the DWP did in respect of my daughter was underscored with a complete lack of respect and care.

"Your daughter has already been down to check her letters," the cleaner said, as she mopped the tiles behind me. "I saw her a little while back.

"It broke my heart to be honest, watching her struggle out of the lift with her walking stick. She didn't look at all well. She could barely walk."

I nodded sadly.

"She's very sick, but she's waiting for an important letter," I explained. "She keeps on checking her pigeonhole down here. Otherwise, she would be in bed."

The day passed again without any contact from the DWP. I made sure Jodey was tucked up in bed before I left her late in the afternoon. That night, I lay awake and restless, and it was no surprise when my phone bleeped with a text at 3am.

"Mam, what am I going to do?"

My heart was heavy. I had been thinking exactly the same thing. And though I replied with assurances, which I did not really believe, the question spun around the insides of my head for hours afterwards. What exactly was she going to do?

It was dawn when I finally slipped into a doze, and then I dreamed that Jodey was stuck in a swamp, up to her neck, with only her head and arms bobbing above the surface. The stench from the water was eye-wateringly rancid, so foul I recoiled from it, even in my sleep. I watched, horrified, as, every now and again, her mouth dipped beneath the surface, and she swallowed great gulps of swamp-water. In one hand, Jodey held a letter, and she was waving it frantically in my direction.

"This is the letter! This is the letter!" she gasped. "Don't let it get wet, Mam, or they won't pay out. Here, can you take it from me?"

In the dream, I was standing on the banking of the swamp, bizarrely wearing the same dress and high shoes I'd bought for Jodey's wedding, so many years earlier. I could feel my high heels sinking into the mud so that I was stuck. I leaned over the edge as far as I could, clamping my hand over my mouth to block out the smell. But I couldn't reach her.

"Don't splash it," she warned. "It must stay dry. They won't pay out, Mam, if it gets wet, please help me."

Teetering on the edge, with my feet still sinking, I just could not grab the letter. I was her mother, and yet I was letting her down. And then I watched, in morbid terror, as the water level rose above her mouth, and then her nose. She was disappearing, right in front of my eyes. I could not save her. When I awoke, my heart was clattering against my ribs. I had to remind myself sternly that it was only a dream, that Jodey was alive and that we would get her benefits back.

"On my way to see you soon," I texted, before stepping into the shower.

Later in the morning, I made the familiar trip to Jodey's. I'd noticed, these past few days, that she was texting me less. I didn't get the usual messages from her whilst I waited at the bus stop, or late at night. She had a lot on her mind, I told myself. That's all it was. Her children had all been rallying too, wanting to visit, offering to help out. They were worried about her, naturally. But to my surprise, when I arrived at Jodey's, she asked me to cancel all her other visitors. It was as if she was withdrawing, bit by bit.

"I can't face it," she told me numbly. "Not when I'm like this. It's not fair on them. I don't want to see anyone but you."

I knew she didn't want to burden her family, to become more of a responsibility than she already was. Even so, it was so unlike Jodey to refuse visits from her children and grandchildren. Normally, she lived for these visits. It was a complete turnaround for her and perhaps it shocked me more than I wanted to admit.

"If you're sure," I said uncertainly. "But I'm certain they'd love to come, if you change your mind."

Deep in a corner of my mind, a warning bell was clanging; louder, louder, louder. But I shut it out and refused to listen. I did not want to see the danger signs. I couldn't bear to follow through with these thoughts. Instead, I wanted to focus on the positives, on the future, and on helping Jodey to get her benefits back. Sweeping my anxieties aside, I set about cleaning her flat and drawing up a list of jobs for the day. Keeping busy was my catharsis. I could only hope it was Jodey's too.

"Right, what's next?" I said, checking my list. "I'm going to call the doctor, see if we can get an appointment for your back."

On top of everything else, she was still having terrible back pains. She couldn't even lie down in her own bed and instead had spent the previous night propped up on the sofa, under a big duvet. The GP receptionist agreed to chase up Jodey's referral to see a spinal consultant.

"See," I said to her. "That's another problem sorted. We'll get there, eventually, Jodey. You and me."

# 8
# Can't Take It Any More

On February 19, I arrived to find her shaking and crying, and she became more dispirited and despairing as the minutes went by. Nothing I said or did seemed to comfort her and by the afternoon, she had worked herself up into a state of complete panic. In the days before, she had often seemed uncommunicative and quite detached, so at first, I was relieved to see a show of emotion from her. She was, after all, only behaving appropriately for her situation. But of course, as always, it didn't stop there with Jodey, and she quickly spiralled.

"I feel like killing myself," she sobbed, plucking at her clothing and her hair. "I can't carry on."

"Don't talk like that," I said sternly. "This is a rough patch, I know, but we'll get through it."

But she became more agitated and irrational and so I decided to call in the mental health crisis team for advice. They offered her a place at Roseberry Park Hospital, the mental health unit. Jodey had been admitted there before, for short periods of time.

"I don't want to go," Jodey said adamantly.

"It won't do me any good. I'm staying here."

I knew better than to try and persuade her.

"That's fine," I said gently. "Nobody will force you."

Instead, a couple of the kids called round, and together we managed to calm her down. By late in the evening, she seemed much better.

"Sorry, Mam," she said quietly.

"You have nothing to apologise for," I said. "It's the DWP at fault here. Not you."

I made my way home, relieved that we had overcome yet another mini crisis. But, if I was honest, I felt we were doing no more than staving off the inevitable. It was like putting one solitary sandbag on the doorstep, knowing there was a tsunami roaring up the road towards us.

"Night Jode," I texted when I got home. "Love you."

"Best mam in the world," she replied.

And how those words warmed my heart.

The next day, February 20, Jodey's postbox was empty again. Still, we had heard nothing about her appeal; not even a phone call. The lack of urgency was another degradation, another ignominy; not only was Jodey not worthy of benefit payments, but neither did she qualify for prompt consideration. I locked the postbox again and climbed the stairs to Jodey's flat. The tension was building in my chest, solid and heavy like a slow-setting cement. If the stress was making me ill like this, I dreaded to think what it was doing to my daughter. After cooking beans on toast for Jodey, changing her bedding, and putting on a wash, I sat at her little dining table, drumming my fingers. My whole body was itching with frustration. Sitting here and waiting passively for a letter was just not good enough. Unable to wait a moment longer, I jumped up as though I'd been poked with a cattle prod.

"I'm going to the Job Centre," I announced. "I'm going to turn up, in person. I'll explain everything. Surely someone will listen."

"Thanks Mam," Jodey smiled.

It was a weary smile, but a smile nonetheless. She had faith in my plan, she had a nugget of hope, and I knew I must not let her down. The Job Centre was a 15-minute walk from Jodey's flat, and I decided it would do me good to try to clear my head. It was a cold and miserable February afternoon, with the clouds hanging low like a curtain of gloomy grey. It felt as though even the sun had given up on us. Even so, as I approached the Job Centre, I felt buoyed and positive. Now that I was here, physically, I felt sure someone would show us some sympathy and understanding. It was a matter of common sense, more than anything, for it was screamingly and heartbreakingly obvious to anyone who knew Jodey that she was unfit to work. I just needed to convey that to the DWP. If I could at least persuade them to reinstate her benefits, temporarily, until she was reassessed, that would be a small victory. These people were human, after all. Weren't they?

There was a security worker, stationed at the door of the Job Centre, and I explained everything to him, as clearly and politely as I could.

"Wait here, please," he said, and he went off to find an assistant.

Again, I started my explanation for her, but she began shaking her head before I had even finished my sentence.

"It sounds as though this case is dormant," she said. "Your daughter would need to come to the Job Centre herself."

"That's the whole point!" I exclaimed, my cheeks flushed with frustration. "Jodey is really unwell. She can't attend an assessment and she can't come to the Job Centre. She certainly can't get a job.

"Can we please have a home visit? Can she have another medical? Can you at least tell me when her appeal will be heard?"

But the assistant simply repeated that the case was dormant. It was like talking to a robot. I tried to fish my stack of DWP letters out of my bag, but she ushered me back towards the door, murmuring useless platitudes. In shock, I found myself back out in the street. She hadn't even bothered looking up Jodey's details on the computer. In fact, she just hadn't taken me seriously at all. I looked through the windows of the Job Centre, at the hands busily typing on keyboards, the blank faces staring at screens. The office was a wall of human misery. It was like dealing with tin men. There was nobody here with a heart.

Trudging back to Jodey's, I felt the bitter cold gnawing at my face. The sun had well and truly disappeared now. There was no warmth left in the world. As I walked, my legs felt heavy and leaden and all at once, I was exhausted. As I neared Jodey's flat, I felt a horrible dread, spreading, like a virus, through my whole body. How on earth would I face her? She had put her faith in me. This was our last hope. I had tried, I had really tried, but it just was not good enough. Drained and jaded, I let myself into her flat. As I turned into the living room, Jodey's face turned expectantly towards me. There was a flicker of hope in her eyes, and it broke my heart. I didn't need to say a word. Instead, I held my hands out, helplessly. The despair was carved right across my face.

"Oh, Mam, what am I going to do?" she whispered. "I can't leave the flat. I can't breathe."

"I know, I know," I said softly. "Don't worry. I will think of something else."

We watched some TV together, a rerun of one of her favourite *Real Housewives* shows, but today somehow the glitz and glamour seemed so superficial, so vulgar. When it was time for my bus home, I said:

"Look, if they don't give you your money back, we will go to the *Gazette*. I will ring them myself. That's what we'll do."

The *Gazette* was our local paper. It was a last resort, but it was all I could think of. And I felt hopeful that, if they contacted the DWP on our behalf, they might be treated with a little more respect. I thought back to the way the assistant at the Job Centre had steered me out onto the street, as though I was a nuisance, a mere idiot, with nothing meaningful to say.

"The *Gazette*," I said again, as I buttoned up my coat. "That's our next hope."

The old Jodey would have laughed and made a quip about getting a make-over before she was prepared to have her photo in the newspaper. She'd have tried on two or three outfits and accessorised one of her handbags. But the new Jodey simply didn't respond. She stared right through me, right past me, and it was an eerie feeling. As I stepped out, into the inky February night, I felt a jolt of anxiety. It was a quiet, sleepy evening, the neighbourhood was calm, and yet my heart was thumping with unease. I looked up at Jodey's third window, lit with a faint blue glow from the TV, and I wished, with all my heart, that there was someone to help us. That night, Jodey's eldest daughter, Louise, called me.

"I've just spoken to Mam and she's agreed to come to my place tomorrow," she said. "I'm worried about her. I'd like to get her out of the flat for a few hours, if I can."

"Me too," I replied.

"I've told Mam I'll send a taxi for her, and she can stay the whole day," Louise continued. "It will give you a break too, Nan. I know you're exhausted."

Much as I hated to admit it, there was a sense of relief to know that I had a day off; time at home where I could catch up on my housework, maybe meet one of my pals for coffee or see my grandchildren. For two years now, I had seen Jodey each day, even twice a day. My life revolved around her and whilst I didn't for a moment resent that or wish it any other way, it was a commitment.

"Thanks Louise," I said. "It will do your mam good too. She needs a change of scene. She hasn't really left her flat for weeks now, except to see the doctor or Citizens Advice."

That night, as I was brushing my ready for bed, my phone bleeped with a message.

"I am going to sleep. I love you Mam."

"You too,' I typed. 'Always."

The next day, Tuesday, February 21 2017, I was up early, washing my windows, scrubbing the floor tiles, and hoovering behind the sofa and the beds. I wanted to be as productive as possible with my free day, but I was also trying to stay busy and steer my mind away from worrying about Jodey. Even though I had a day off from my unofficial caring duties, I couldn't help thinking of her constantly. And though

I had vowed not to bother her whilst she was with Louise, my hands were twitching just to give her a quick call. The worry gnawed and chewed at me all day, and yet there was no real reason for it. I knew she was safe with Louise. Besides, Jodey was no doubt looking forward to having a break from me – she had seen so much of me recently! I didn't want to call and spoil that for her. But by early evening, before I started cooking, I could wait no longer.

"I'll just give her a quick ring," I decided. "Say hello. Nothing more."

First, I called Jodey. But her phone rang out, again and again. That wasn't unusual, I told myself, she was probably having a nap on the sofa. I peeled the potatoes and carrots and set them to boil. Then, I called again. Still nothing. I wondered whether she'd decided to stay over with Louise. It would be lovely for them both if that was the case. I called my granddaughter and she picked up immediately.

"Oh, Mam didn't come," she told me. "She didn't get in the taxi this morning. She said she was ill, so I haven't seen her all day. I'm sorry, Nan. I thought she was going to let you know."

"No," I said faintly, clutching the door frame for reassurance. "No, I've not heard a thing from her."

I hung up and tried to steady myself, taking deep breaths. My knees were buckling, and I was seized by a sharp shot of anxiety. Yet it was odd; I felt no actual shock. Instead, a pervading sense of doom and dread sluiced through me. I tried calling Jodey again and again. Deep down, I had a horrible, sickly feeling. A realisation that my world was about to turn and flip and shatter. There was no real reason to panic; it was perfectly possible that

Jodey might be in bed, fast asleep. Yet somehow, I felt it was more than that. Recent snapshots flashed through my mind: Jodey refusing to have her photo taken on my birthday, Jodey numb and mute when I promised to call the newspaper; Jodey staring ahead, fixedly, at nothing. She had even spelled it out, directly and brutally:

*I feel like killing myself!*

But I had dismissed her words as just another impulsive outburst, wild and unsubstantiated. I wouldn't – couldn't – believe that she was serious. Yet all of these had been red alerts, I realised that now. The warning bells which I had tried so hard to ignore clanged noisily right behind my eye sockets. My head pounded as I called the concierge of Jodey's block.

"I'll try her intercom," he offered. "Just give me a moment."

The line was silent except for my own jagged breathing.

"I'm sorry," he said. "No reply from your daughter's intercom. I would call the police if you're concerned."

I hung up and dialled the police immediately.

"I'm worried about my daughter," I explained. "I can't get hold of her. I wondered if you could send someone round to check on her, please."

"Perhaps she's gone out," the officer suggested.

"No way," I replied. "She's unwell. She's too ill to leave her home. She never goes out. Besides, she has absolutely no money. Where would she go?"

The officer seemed to be making a note of everything I said and the minutes were dragging by. Inwardly, I was screaming: 'Please hurry! Please check on her!'

"So would you like to report her missing?" he asked eventually.

"Not really," I hesitated. "I don't think she's missing. I think she's in her flat. But I'm concerned for her safety."

"Well, you would have to file a report before we can act," he replied.

"Right, okay, let's get started," I said impatiently. "This is urgent."

It wasn't his fault, I knew that. But my exasperation was mounting.

"I'm afraid I'll have to get someone to call you back," he said. "We'll be as quick as we can."

I could barely believe it. I left my details and hung up. By now, I was too uneasy to even think about eating. I switched off the pans and then paced the living room, my mind whirling, worrying I was overreacting, worrying I was underreacting. I didn't know what to do for the best. I felt as though my judgement was clouded; was this an emergency, or simply a misunderstanding? Perhaps Jodey would call me at any minute with a straightforward explanation.

"Sorry Mam, phone was on silent! Been watching back-to-back *Cheshire Housewives*!"

Every so often I glared at my phone, urging it to ring. When it bleeped with a message, even though I was expecting it, I jumped out of my skin.

"Have you heard from Mam?" Louise texted.

"No," I replied. "I'm waiting for the police to call me back."

"I'm going to the flat myself," Louise messaged. "I need to see what's going on."

I arranged to meet her there, with the spare key, as soon as I could. I bitterly regretted contacting the police now, because it was slowing me down. To distract myself,

I flicked on the kettle and threw a tea bag into a mug. And as I was getting the milk out of the fridge, my phone rang. I hoped against hope that it might be Jodey, but instead there was a police officer on the other end. Painstakingly, he took Jodey's details, and every question he asked seemed to last an hour. My heart was beating faster and faster and I could feel a sheen of cold sweat forming across my face.

"Look, I really need to go and check on her," I stuttered. "I've arranged to meet my granddaughter. I'm sorry but I'll have to go."

I hung up and grabbed my spare key. It was cold and dark outside with a faint mist curling around my face like cold fingers. It was a typically bleak and miserable February evening. I had called a cab, despite the expense, because I couldn't bear to wait for the bus. Not now. I had the strongest sense that I was running out of time, yet I didn't know why. Even so, it was after 10pm when the cab pulled up outside Jodey's block. Louise met me in the foyer, along with the concierge.

"Oh Nan," she said tearfully.

I squeezed her hand, not trusting myself to speak. I took the stairs, thinking that they would be quicker than waiting for the lifts. It was only three floors, yet tonight, it felt like an endless climb. I thought of all the times I had used these stairs; carrying shopping, prescriptions and takeaway treats. Often, I was filled with excitement, desperate to share a snippet of gossip with Jodey. Other times, I was exhausted and ready to enjoy a bag of chips on her sofa. But tonight, all I felt was panic. White panic, blaring in my brain like a siren, blotting out everything else. Eventually I arrived at Jodey's flat and, with shaking hands, I fumbled my key into the lock. At the same time, I rapped on the door and shouted:

"Jodey! It's Mam, love. Let me in!"

Nothing. The silence cut right through me like a blade. I took a deep breath, leaned down and opened the letterbox.

"Jodey! Please! Come on!"

Nothing.

My heart was thrashing now, ricocheting around my ribs, bursting out of my chest. For some reason, the key wouldn't turn. I took it out, examined it, tried it again. This was the same key I had used for two years, to let myself into my daughter's flat, every day. But now, inexplicably, terrifyingly, it would not work. It did not want to work. My mind raced irrationally; I became convinced the key was trying to tell me something, that it wanted to protect me. From what?

"Help!" I yelled. "Someone please help me with this key!"

Within moments, the concierge was at my shoulder.

"Here, let me try," he said kindly.

He took my key and I watched, dumbstruck, how he opened the door easily first time. He walked into Jodey's flat, and I followed. The flat was in darkness. I tried to swallow but there was a marble lodged in my throat and my whole body tingled with dread.

"Jodey," I pleaded. "Are you there, love? Please?"

The concierge was just a few steps ahead in the darkened hallway but suddenly, as he opened the door to the living room and flicked on the light, he froze.

"Stand back, Mrs Dove," he said, putting his arm out as a barrier. "Step back. Please."

I heard the words, but I could not process them. My legs propelled me relentlessly forwards, as though I was being operated by remote control. A voice in my head was screaming at me to turn around, turn around and run away as fast as I could. But my legs kept on walking. I was her mother. I had to be here. I could not let her down.

"Stand back," he said again.

I heard the horror in his voice, but he sounded faraway, distant. I focused only on moving forwards. I was maybe six steps away from the living room door, but it seemed to take hours, light years, until I reached the doorway. And then, as I rounded the corner, I saw her.

"No," I screamed. "No! No! No!"

Falling to my knees, I clamped my hands over my mouth to stifle my screams. But nothing could silence me.

*'If anything happens to me, Mam, don't be screaming...'*

Had she known, even then, on our shopping trip that this was going to happen? Had she known she would die? And had she known I would scream?

Jodey was sitting upright and stiff on the sofa, dressed in black leggings and a black T-shirt. All in black. Her face was waxy pale, one eye was closed, one was open; glassy, unseeing, yet that familiar dazzling blue. As I ran towards her, I thought I saw a single tear roll slowly down her cheek. One last, lonely, tear. She had a bandage on her leg, and it had been troubling her for days. Everything was so normal, so instantly recognisable, and yet at once so grotesque and completely alien. Strewn all over the carpet were sheets of writing paper, surrounding Jodey like a flock of little white birds. Amongst them were blister packets of pills, all empty. On the table were empty bottles of Oramorph. With my head in my hands, I screamed and screamed.

*Mam. 'Don't be screaming.'*

Someone was ushering me into the hallway, and out of the flat. A paramedic, a nice young man with a kind face, said:

"I think she's been dead for quite some time. I'm so sorry. Can we ask you to wait outside for a while?"

Like a zombie, I called Eric and Jamie. My voice, when I spoke, came as a strangled sob.

"Who is that?" Jamie asked. "Mam? Is that you?"

It broke my heart to form the words, knowing that at the end of my sentence, his life, like mine, would be shattered.

"It's Jodey," I wept. "She's gone, Jamie. We've lost her."

We took the lift back down to the foyer, and a couple got in alongside us.

"Something awful has happened on the third floor," one said to me. "God knows what."

Downstairs, the concierge found us some chairs. One by one, Jodey's children and her close friends began arriving. Jamie came too. Donna's phone was switched off and I couldn't get hold of her and really, I didn't want to. I didn't want to break her heart. A police officer took me aside and explained that as Jodey's next of kin, I would need to make a statement. I nodded numbly. I told him everything I could but knowing nothing would bring her back. Afterwards, he suggested we might like a few moments with Jodey, before the undertakers arrived.

"You might want to spend those last few minutes with her in her home," he suggested.

I was so grateful. Together with my granddaughters, we pushed her favourite fluffy slippers onto her feet, and we draped her dressing gown around her shoulders. Jodey had always felt the cold.

"That will keep you nice and warm, pet," I said softly.

The papers on the floor had by now been picked up by the police, photographed and categorised. Each one was a letter; from Jodey to me and all of her children. The eldest was 25, the youngest, just 16. She had written letters of love to us all. There was also a letter – entitled 'The Life Of Jodey Whiting' – which confirmed she had taken her own life, aged 42. She had written:

"I have no money, I can't walk, I can't breathe, I want peace. I can't take it any more."

Clutching the letter to my heart, I sobbed.

"I know," I whispered. "I know, Jodey."

The undertakers arrived and advised us to leave the flat.

"You won't want to be here whilst we prepare your daughter's body," they said.

But I couldn't leave the building, I couldn't just walk away. I had to be there for her now, just as I always had been. I waited in the corridor until Jodey's body was carried out, covered respectfully with a body bag. I ran towards her and placed my hand on the surface, where I thought her hand might be.

"I'm here," I whispered, walking alongside her, as she was wheeled into the lift and then out again. "I won't leave you."

As we walked through the foyer, I had a flashback to Jodey as a little girl, in a busy shopping precinct one Saturday afternoon.

"Hold my hand!" I cried. "You're going to get lost!"

"I'll never get lost!" she giggled as she held out her small hand and curled her fingers around mine. I remembered the warmth of her hand and her mouth sticky with penny sweets and her white socks pulled up to her knees. She was lost now, my little Jodey-Podey. She was gone forever.

We reached the hearse, in the car park outside, and the undertaker waited for me to step back. But as I lifted my hand from her body, I felt as though I was letting her down; I was letting her go. My throat closed around a silent scream as it drove away.

*'Mam. Don't be screaming.'*

* * *

At around 1.30am, I went, with Jamie, to Eric's house. The pain was so intense, so wounding, that I truly believed I might die myself that night. We waited in silence for the sun to come up and then I went to see Donna.

"I'm sorry, love," I said, as she opened the door, her face registering surprise and then concern at my early visit. "Jodey has gone."

"What was it, her breathing?" Donna asked, the tears streaming down her cheeks. "Was it pneumonia?"

I shook my head.

"It looks like she took her own life," I said sadly. "She couldn't take any more. She had no money, no hope, no future."

It was a double blow for Donna, having to accept that Jodey was dead and that she had taken her own life.

"It didn't need to happen, Mam," Donna said fiercely. "She was made to feel like an outcast, like a burden on society. She felt worthless. That's what killed my sister."

I nodded. Donna was right. Despite all her physical ailments, Jodey had died from shame. From Donna's, I made my way back home. As I walked inside, I spotted the milk carton on the work surface and the mug with the tea bag inside. My head swam. As I stared at the kettle, time seemed to collapse and shrink. Less than 24 hours earlier, I'd been about to make a cup of tea, believing then that Jodey was alive. The cup was still waiting. The tea bag was there. But Jodey was dead. Nothing had changed, and yet everything had changed. The pan of boiled potatoes waited idly on the sink. How could that be? How could everything in the world remain the same, without my beloved Jodey in it? I felt a sudden fury towards the tea bag, the potatoes, the carton of milk. How could they carry on as normal, without her?

Wearily, with every bone aching, I lay on my bed, fully clothed. But I knew I would not sleep. My whole body howled with emptiness, and I felt I would never know peace again. That final scene with Jodey played on a loop inside my head; round and round, me telling her that the Job Centre had refused to listen, her crushed, broken, unable to take it in:

*Oh, Mam, what am I going to do? I can't leave the flat. I can't breathe.*

Jodey had her problems, I knew that. She had battled bravely, almost her entire life, with one health setback after another. But she had deteriorated very sharply since her benefits were stopped. Mentally, she had been teetering over a cliff edge ever since she got that first letter informing her that she had missed her assessment. Now, after weeks without benefits, weeks without money, she had plunged to her death. Surrounded by concentric circles of debt, worry and pain, she could finally take no more. I was in no doubt, none at all, that with her benefits in place, Jodey would still have been alive. Eventually, I gave up on sleep and I went for a walk. I dreaded seeing any of my friends or neighbours; they always asked after Jodey. Everyone cared about Jodey. Everyone except the DWP. The girl from Benefits Street had been killed by a lack of benefits. The irony was abhorrent.

Later that day, I met up with Eric and the children, to read through the letters that she had left. My own letter was in my coat pocket, carefully folded. It was precious to me – priceless even – and yet I could not bring myself to look at it. Only when Donna was with me, my hand in hers, did I feel strong enough to unfold it at last. As I spread the page on my knee, I recognised the paper; on our last shopping trip, she had bought a bag of little books and diaries to give out as Christmas gifts. Evidently, she had kept one of the books back and used it to write her suicide notes. As I began to read, quite out of the blue, the lights flickered overhead. And then again.

"That's Jodey," Donna smiled. "She's keeping an eye on us. You know what she's like if she's not involved."

I steadied myself to begin reading. Even with Jodey's spirit holding me together, it was hard.

"Mam," she wrote. "I love u so much. You r my legend. Plz keep my babys safe plz mam. Always watch ova them. I'm at peace with Nanna. I will always watch ova u all. Xx"

Through my tears, I smiled at her spelling and grammar mistakes. Typical Jodey. There was a hotch-potch of emotion and pain, spilled right across the page. I imagined her writing the letters all alone, her mind fuddled by the overdose, her heart splintering with every word. She must have been so afraid in those final hours, and so lonely too. And yet, part of me still didn't believe she was gone. Even though I had the note, even though I had seen her body, I just could not accept it. Another note read:

"Help my kids have a gud life...I've had to do this cause I've had enough of my life I don't want to go on, on earth. I will be with Nanna Chetham and my family who have passed. I will fly n b watching you all. Love you Mam."

Nanna Chetham was my own mother, and Jodey had always adored her. The children were all busy reading their letters, Donna and Jamie and Eric had theirs. There were open letters too, addressed to us all. I was trying to build myself up to reading them when a picture unexpectedly fell from the wall and clattered onto the carpet.

"That's Jodey again," Donna said, with an attempt at a smile. "You know how she hates to be left out."

One page was filled with chaotic scribble. But as I read it, I got a real sense of how wretched Jodey felt at that moment, of how the despair was dragging her in and dragging her under.

"I need help. support. not being able 2 walk anywhere without getting very bad pain in my back. weak. Need support. Mobility scooter. March hospital appointment. I don't have a life. I can't walk, breathe..."

Another page read:

"Want to sort but no credit. No muni. Xmas just want presents for family. Couldn't pay bills. No food..."

And then, in desperate, screaming, capital letters:

"I'VE HAD ENOUGH."

It was too much for me and I broke down, sobbing. Jodey had laid her soul bare, she had begged and pleaded for help, but she had been shunned, ignored, and kicked aside. I could not imagine that a stray animal would have been treated worse.

With a grim face, Jamie handed me a letter which read:

'I hope sum 1 will love my twins…Cory is gonna end up dead…I av 2 go 2 b waiting 4 him. God forbid tho.'

I felt a chill run through me. Jodey seemed to be predicting Cory's death in this letter. I told myself that she was probably very confused and very drugged, and that it meant nothing. But I remembered her warning:

*'Mam. Don't be screaming'*

And the accuracy pierced me to the bone. What if this was another chilling prophecy? I made a secret vow to keep a special watch over Cory.

The following day, I took the bus to the coroner's office in Middlesbrough, to find out when we could expect to have Jodey's body returned to us to plan her funeral. But everything seemed such an effort. Even walking to the bus stop took much longer than usual. That short journey felt as though I was wading through sludge and my bones ached and creaked, as though they, too, were weeping for Jodey.

"Can I bring my daughter home, where she belongs?" I asked the coroner's assistant.

I was told that it would be several days before Jodey's body was released to the undertakers, and only then could we begin organising the funeral. I hated the idea of her being in a morgue. The thought of her being cold, above all else, upset me. I wanted to ask the assistant to make sure she was wrapped up warm, but I knew it would make no sense. Nothing made sense anymore.

As I waited for the bus home, I felt an almost magnetic pull towards Jodey's flat. It seemed incomprehensible to me that she was no longer there. I had just been told that her body was in the morgue and yet part of me wanted to get off at her stop and check; just to be sure that there was no mistake. And that night, I lay on my bed, again fully clothed, with sleep far away, clutching my phone in my hand. Silently, I pleaded for one last message from her. One last sign. Anything.

*'Can't sleep Mam. U awake?'*

I checked and re-checked my phone. And when, finally, I drifted into a doze, I heard phantom bleeps in my sleep. *Message from Jodey! She's here after all!* I awoke to one glorious moment of joy before being plunged back into an eviscerating pain. As it grew light, I showered and changed and went to the Citizens Advice office.

"You might remember, I came to see you with my daughter, Jodey," I began.

"Yes, of course," Susan said, frowning as she noticed my tears. "What's happened?"

I could hardly bring myself to say the words.

"I need your help, please," I sobbed.

It was almost harder to say the three letters: DWP. As I spoke, I felt such a rage ripping through me, that it frightened me. It was a spitting, swirling, murderous rage; something I had never felt myself capable of before.

"She died without ever winning her appeal," I said. "She never even got a reply."

Susan shook her head.

"I will inform the DWP of Jodey's death," she told me. "In fact, I'll do it right now, whilst you're here."

I waited whilst she made a phone call and afterwards, she said:

"All departments will be notified immediately. There is a system called: 'Tell Us Once' so that you won't have to go through this with anyone else."

"Thank you," I replied. "But now that she's dead, I don't want this to be swept under the carpet. I want to fight this, for Jodey's sake. I want people to know how the DWP treated her."

Susan suggested I could take up the appeal as Jodey's appointee. She helped me to fill in the paperwork and she promised to help me as much as she could. I was touched by her compassion, especially since it jarred so sharply with the contempt the DWP had shown us.

"You're not on your own," Susan said, as I stood up to leave. "Don't ever forget that."

Later that day, a post-mortem revealed, as expected, that Jodey had died from an overdose of her prescription drugs: morphine, amitriptyline and pregabalin. The medication that was supposed to help her had in fact killed her in the end.

"Can we see her yet?" I asked.

The undertaker explained it would take another couple of days before they were ready for us to visit. My heart ached just to look at her face, to hold her hand, one last time. Though her image hovered constantly in front of me, like a mirage, I was frightened that I might soon forget it. I needed to see her again, to fix the picture in my mind for safe-keeping.

On February 25, only four days after Jodey's death, I went to her flat to collect her mail. It was horrible, making that journey, walking into the foyer as I had so many hundreds of times in the past. Today, though, I wasn't carrying shopping or prescriptions or a warm casserole. I was carrying only my broken heart.

I opened Jodey's mailbox, and, like a burning coal, glowing in the gloom, there it was. The letter from the DWP. I recognised the slim brown envelope before I had even touched it. The timing seemed so cruel. How could they send this when they had already been notified that she was dead? It felt as though it had been done on purpose, though I knew that was unlikely to be the case, because nobody at the DWP applied that amount of thought to Jodey. Ripping it open, I began to read, and I felt my heart constricting sharply. My face hardened in sheer disbelief, as if my features were turning to stone.

"We have taken into account all the information available," said the letter. "We have not changed our decision... I am unable to revise the decision of 6.02.17... this is because you have not provided good cause for your failure to attend a medical examination on 16.01.17....as a result you are not entitled to Employment and Support Allowance. ...

"I do not consider that any exceptional circumstances apply to you."

I sank down on a bench in the foyer. My tears rained down onto the page, blurring the words. According to the DWP, Jodey was fit to work, even as her body lay cold in the morgue.

# 9

# The Fight Goes On

Over those few days, I barely slept and when I did, I dreamed of Jodey. I ate virtually nothing, surviving on tea and coffee and half a mug of soup, here and there. I told myself not to dwell on the letter from DWP, because it would simply have made me bitter and ill and I had more pressing issues to concentrate on, such as planning my daughter's funeral. Yet it was impossible not to replay those words round and round my head. The injustice and the insensitivity hung heavy on me, like a cloak made of concrete. I could not simply let this go.

*'We have not changed our decision. ...I am unable to revise the decision of 6.02.17...'*

At the end of that week, we were finally allowed to see Jodey at the Chapel of Rest. Her coffin was white with roses painted around the handles and my first thought, when I saw it, was that she would have loved it. Jodey was dressed in her favourite blue flowery pyjamas, her blue dressing gown and slippers. Like me, her favourite colour was blue, and I always felt there was a synchronicity there, especially with Jodey's bright blue eyes. It was a comfort to me, silly I know, that she was dressed warmly and cosily in the coffin.

It mattered so much. The undertaker, Irene Jessop, had done Jodey's hair and make-up beautifully, and had placed a single white rose in her hand.

As I leaned over the coffin side, I was suddenly ambushed by a memory from nearly 40 years ago, and it was so clear, so real, that it took my breath away. Jodey was only around four years old, and we were visiting friends. Jodey and Donna were playing in the garden outside, with my friend's older children, when Donna came rushing into the house to tell me Jodey had slipped out of the garden and disappeared. We all ran outside in a panic, calling her name and trying to find her. When we eventually spotted her, she was next door, happily picking rose petals from their garden, one by one, and popping them into her pockets. She turned to me, without a care in the world, and said:

"Mammy, look at these lovely flowers! They smell so nice!"

She had always loved roses, ever since then. I focused again on the rose in her hand and blinked away my tears.

"You look beautiful," I told her softly. "Really stunning, pet."

I moved her hair to frame her face a little, the way she liked it. And I popped a bag of rainbow drops and an energy drink into the coffin with her.

"Just in case you get peckish," I smiled, patting her cheek. "I'll be back tomorrow, don't you worry."

I visited the next afternoon, and the next, keeping her up to date with all the news and the gossip, especially the latest scoops from the Reality Housewives shows she loved.

"Oh, you should have seen her shoes," I said to her. "Red, high heels with jewels up the side. You would have wanted a pair for yourself, Jode, I can tell you.

"And don't get me started on the Botox! I just don't get it."

Each morning, as I rushed through my housework before going to the undertakers, I could almost convince myself that I was off to see Jodey in her flat and that nothing really had changed.

As the days passed, her coffin filled with sweets and treats and trinkets and favourite photos. Her children had a necklace made with all their names on. It was a mark of how much she was loved, in how many tributes she received.

"They'll struggle to carry that coffin with all that luggage inside," I joked to Jodey. "You might want to think about hiring some muscle."

Next to her coffin, the undertakers had placed a large white candle, with a verse on the front:

'In Loving Memory of Jodey Whiting.
Time is not measured by the years that you live
But by the deeds that you do and the joy that you give
And each day as it comes brings a chance to each one
To live to the fullest, leaving nothing undone.'

I tried to draw comfort from those words, but it was hard. We had started our plans for the funeral, and it was important to me that my daughter had a good send-off, because that day would be my final gift to her. As her mother, I wanted to make sure that she had a day to remember. But of course, as always, money was at the heart of it. We were advised that the funeral would cost an estimated £4,500 with a further £2,000 for the headstone. As a pensioner, I had no earnings, and no savings. I applied for an emergency grant from the DWP but my application was refused, almost immediately. Their heartlessness by now did not surprise me at all and it certainly did not deter me.

"I'll find a way," I said defiantly, scrunching the letter and the brown envelope into the bin. "She's having a nice funeral, and that's that."

Donna was with me, and she smiled.

"Do you ever wonder where our Jodey got that stubborn streak?" she asked.

It was embarrassing explaining my situation to the undertakers, but I was prepared to do whatever it took to make Jodey's final day special. And they were very kind, agreeing to let me pay the bill off as and when I could manage it. Eric and Jodey's children all chipped in to help too.

Her funeral was arranged for March 10 at St Bede's Chapel, at Teesside Crematorium, followed by burial at Thornaby cemetery. She had requested burial in the letters written before her death, because she wanted somewhere the children could visit and feel close to her. We had a beautiful order of service printed, with a photo of Jodey smiling, and a verse saying:

*Goodbye my family my life is past, I loved you all to the very last,*
*Weep not for me, but courage take, love each other, for my sake,*
*For those you love don't go away,*
*They walk beside you every day.*

Donna had offered to have Jodey's body at her house on the night before the service, so that we could all spend one last evening with her. The undertaker, who had been so compassionate towards us, agreed immediately. We all crowded at Donna's window as though we were waiting for a royal visit, and when we saw the hearse arriving outside the house, there was a collective ripple of emotion. I heard muffled sobs around me, but I felt a little swell of joy too, as though Jodey was coming home to us. I wanted to feel close to her again. The coffin was wheeled through the front door and into Donna's back room and then the lid was opened.

"Welcome back, Jode," I whispered.

At first, everyone kept a respectful distance from the coffin, nobody really knowing exactly what was the correct or appropriate thing to do. Jodey's favourite films were running on DVD and we played all her favourite songs too; they were mainly the old ones from her teenage years; Madonna and Michael Jackson. I remembered her and Debbie dancing around the bedroom singing, music blasting. They had been such happy days. In the background, one of the grand-children began peering over the side of the coffin.

"Nanna!" he lisped. "Nanna!"

I smiled at the curiosity on his face, and I went to hug him, realising this was Jodey's way of telling us she felt left out. She had never been one to sit quietly in the corner of the room, and neither should she now.

"This is Jodey's night," I said. "Let's do her make-up, style her hair, get her ready for tomorrow."

One by one, the kids all got involved, trying different lipsticks, new colours of eyeshadow. Someone brushed her hair. Someone else straightened her clothes.

"She'd love this," I said to myself. "She'd be so cross to miss her own party."

Donna had daffodils growing in her front garden and she picked out a bunch to put in the coffin. Jodey looked beautiful, framed by flowers and gifts. She looked younger somehow, all her worry lines were gone, all the stress of her illnesses and her DWP battle had been ironed out, as if by magic. She was back to being carefree, back to being her old self, as if her death had turned back time.

"My Jodey-Podey," I smiled.

All night, we took it in turns to stay awake with her, so that she was not alone. This was what she had always wanted, her family back under one roof, together again at last. Tragically, it had taken her death to grant her dearest wish. All through the early hours, through the darkest time before the dawn, I sat by her coffin, reliving the old days:

"Remember the time you marched into school to sort out that lad who was bullying our Jamie?"

"And what about that day you helped yourself to a bag of baby clothes and pretended they were rubbish!"

"Or the time the doctor chased us out of the surgery waving his shoe because you wouldn't stop wailing!"

It was quiet in the back room, but I fancied I could hear Jodey giggling softly at the memories. As first light came, in a pink and orange sky, I typed out one last text:

"U awake Jodey? Mam here. Love you to the moon and back."

\* \* \*

Soon after, my Jodey was driven away for the final time, in a beautiful horse-drawn carriage. And though I had prepared myself and steadied myself, I could not believe, would not believe, that this was the last goodbye. It pained me that Jodey was missing her own funeral; I know it was a silly thought, but she would have loved the day. Still so much an animal lover, she'd have fussed over the horses pulling the carriage, and she'd have been wowed by the style and the extravagance of the procession. The streets were lined with mourners, who cried and clapped as the cortege drove past. Jodey would have enjoyed that too. She had asked, in her final letters, for everyone to wear bright colours, and I had bought a black and purple outfit which was quite a statement, and exactly her taste. I could almost hear her as I slipped the lacy top over my head.

*Mam, you look a picture! Doesn't half suit you!*

She had chosen her own songs too: *The Final Countdown* by Europe, *Freedom* by QFX, and *I Don't Wanna Live Forever* by Taylor Swift and Zayn Malik. They were all songs about escaping pain, about a new beginning. I hoped desperately that she would be at peace now, that her second chance, wherever it was, would be a happy one. Then, as we left the church, she had picked: *Always Look on the Bright Side of Life*. That was Jodey's cheeky streak, shining through, right at the end. I felt a glimmer of warmth inside as the music began to play, as though she was with me, still.

She was later buried in the same cemetery as my grandfather, James Conlon. He had died when I was eight months' pregnant with Jodey, and so they had never met. It was a small shred of comfort to me that they could be together at last.

That afternoon, there were hundreds of mourners at the wake, which was held in a local pub. Jodey's old friends right back to primary school and high school were there. Some were people I hadn't seen for many years. With each introduction, each conversation, came a fresh wave of tears. I could not believe I still had tears left to cry. One man tapped me on the elbow and explained he was a support worker at the hostel where Jodey had lived briefly after her marriage broke down.

"I never forgot Jodey," he smiled. "She had a lovely way about her. She had her own problems, but I ended up telling her my life story! She was like the mother figure in that place."

"That sounds typical of her," I agreed.

As it grew late, some of Jodey's children returned to the cemetery, to be with her. The thought of her being left out was awful, and I wanted to go too, but I wasn't sure my legs would hold me up much longer.

"Let them go," Jamie said to me. "You've had one hell of a day, Mam. I think you should get to bed."

He called a taxi and saw me safely inside my flat. After he had gone, and the silence fell around me, I sank onto the sofa and my eyes swam with yet more tears. My Jodey was gone. Fragile and feisty in equal measure, she'd had the rest of her life ahead of her; wrapped in a warm blanket of familial love. Yet that did not save her. Yet we could not reach her.

"Jodey," I whispered helplessly. "Jodey, love. Why did you leave me?"

The silence was thick and stifling. And then, quite extraordinarily, the bulb above me popped and plunged me into darkness.

"Jodey!" I smiled, pulling myself up off the sofa. "You always have to have the last word. Always!"

During the night, I rolled over, more than half-asleep, and felt someone take hold of my left hand.

"Jodey!" I exclaimed, snapping wide-awake.

I flicked on the bedside light and examined my hands in front of me. Of course there was nothing there. But there was a faint impression on the skin of my left hand, slightly moist too, as though someone else's hand had been in mine. I had felt her, I was certain.

I fell back to sleep but then, through my dreams, I heard her shouting, pleading for help.

"Mam! Don't leave me! Don't let me die!"

This time, when I opened my eyes, I was drenched with sweat and sobbing. I felt sure that I'd heard Jodey in those final moments, appealing for help, wishing that someone might find her before it was too late. Her cries rung still in my ears, even though I was awake, and I knew I wouldn't get back to sleep. Instead, I flicked on the kettle and sat in my armchair, tortured by my thoughts. I wondered whether Jodey had expected me to check on her earlier than I did. Perhaps she thought I would be there to save her? I remembered the day of her death, how I'd kept myself busy, how I'd not called her, how I'd believed she was safe. All that time, she was suffering, she was alone, she was dying. I could not escape the belief that she had cried for me, in those final moments. She had shouted my name and I was not there.

Later in the morning, I shook off the remaining cobwebs from my dreams, with the intent of channelling my grief into something more practical. Filled with resolve and fight, and using the advice from Citizens Advice, I filed an appeal on Jodey's behalf, to HM Courts and Tribunals, against the decision from DWP.

"I won't let this go, Jode," I said as I dropped my envelope into the postbox. "I'll keep fighting, no matter what."

It was a little over two weeks before I received the news that the original decision by the DWP had been overturned. We had won our appeal. Quite incredibly, the decision was made on Jamie's birthday, March 31. I knew it was coincidental, but the timing could not have been worse.

As I read the letter, I felt winded. It was now accepted that there was a good reason for Jodey not to have attended the assessment on January 16. Each word felt like a shard of glass, right through my lungs. Jodey would now – had she been alive – be eligible for benefits after all. This was no victory, no celebration for me. If anything, it rubbed salt into my already raw and bleeding wounds. It had taken the DWP three months to see sense, and in that time, my daughter had lost her life. The crass insensitivity of the timing was one thing. But howling back at me, from the page, was the message that Jodey need not have died. This letter, if it had come earlier, would have saved her. The whole horrific tragedy had been triggered by a DWP mistake.

"A mistake!" I gasped when I called Donna. "Can you believe it? Jodey's whole life has been written off because of an error. Nine kids without a mother because someone ticked the wrong box. A mother, a daughter, a sister lost. It's not right. It's really not right."

I felt a growing sense of injustice which cut deeper as time went on. I had thought that Jodey's death was the worst thing that could happen to me. But no; living without Jodey, missing her, was so much harder.

* * *

Early in April, I received a back-payment of £373.80 in benefits from the DWP, on Jodey's behalf. *Blood money.* It might as well have been 30 pieces of silver.

"I don't want this," I snapped. "It can go to charity. It is too little, too late. It's a slap in the face."

Three days after the payment came, I made a formal complaint to the DWP, again with the help of the wonderful Citizens Advice, detailing all that had gone wrong since January.

"I cannot and will not accept that people are treated without humanity, without dignity, and without decency," I said.

I tried to concentrate on my complaint, to give me some focus. But those days, through April and into May, seemed to merge and glue together. My whole routine was shattered; my daily visits to see Jodey, my trips to the shops, to the Job Centre, to the GP surgery. Everything had revolved around her. Now, everything had stopped. It was like severing a main artery. I had invested so much time and love into Jodey and I felt as though my reason for existence had been snatched from me. I wasn't eating or sleeping, and I found myself, more often than not, in floods of tears. The family all did their best to keep me going, and of course I was lucky to have them around me, but I was painfully aware that they were battling with their own anguish too. We were all in mourning. And though I tried to support them – as they did me – we were all swimming against a great tide of suffering, all smothered and suffocated by our sadness. Besides, a part of me didn't want to feel better; how could I enjoy life, how could I ever be happy again, knowing that my daughter was cold in the ground? It felt like a betrayal, every time I felt myself smile.

And there was a terrible sense of guilt and reproach too. I went over and over Jodey's final days. Every time I closed my eyes, I saw her face, blank and expressionless, her shoulders slumped with defeat. The red flags were there. She had been slowly giving up, withdrawing from life. Why did I not see those warnings, or rather, why did I not see them for what they were? In truth, I'd thought that if I was positive and proactive, then my enthusiasm would somehow be infectious. I thought I could save my daughter with love and care alone. But I was wrong. In those final days of her life. I was frightened of addressing the issue of suicide with Jodey, worried that I might in some way put the idea in her head, worried I might lead her down the wrong path. In reality, I was probably most afraid of what her answer might be. Instead, I had kidded myself and I had clung to hope, even when no hope remained. I did not want to believe that my daughter would ever actually kill herself – no mother wants to accept that. No mother likes to think that she is not enough.

Most of all, the memory of my final trip to the Job Centre, to plead on her behalf, was lodged in my mind like a sharp stone rattling around my skull. I could not forget the way Jodey had looked at me when I returned empty handed. Her eyes were empty and lost. For her, the battle was over at that point. It was only looking back now, with the painful clarity of hindsight, that I could see that.

And on the day itself, when I had kept myself busy dusting and polishing, my poor daughter had been alone and desperate, swallowing tablets whilst she poured her heart out on scraps of cheap paper. I was flooded with recriminations, turning those final hours over and over in my mind, wondering whether, if we had found her sooner, she might have been saved. Many nights, through the darkness, I heard Jodey crying out for me. It tore me in two.

I would carry my own share of responsibility for the rest of my life, as any mother would. But in more rational moments I knew that I had done my best for Jodey and that I carried no blame at all for her death. There were others, though, who needed to be held to account. Others who had held her life in their hands and discarded it without a moment's thought. And, as my thoughts slowly settled and crystallised, my sorrow turned, again, to anger.

"This isn't fair," I told Donna, again and again. "Jodey didn't need to die. She shouldn't have been pushed to this."

An inquest into Jodey's death had been opened and adjourned after her death and we were advised it would be several months before it was held. In desperation, I wrote a letter to the coroner, outlining my grievances with the DWP, and asking her to investigate. I also wrote to the *Gazette*, our local paper, asking them to cover the inquest. It had been my final promise to Jodey that I would ask the *Gazette* to run her story. This was not how I had planned it, but I fully intended to keep my promise. I filed an appeal too against the DWP decision against helping to pay for Jodey's funeral. It was in some way cathartic, writing it all down. With a stack of letters waiting, I got wrapped up and walked to the postbox. It was a bitter morning, with a breeze whipping around every street corner, and I could almost hear Jodey's voice, carrying on the wind.

*Doing a grand job there, Mam. Knew you wouldn't let me down.*

"But I did let you down," I mumbled in reply. "I just can't shake that feeling."

\* \* \*

We had agreed with the council that we would remove all of Jodey's belongings from her flat, ready for the next tenant. It was a necessary task, but I was dreading it all the same. Jamie made several trips back and forth in his car, distributing furniture and keepsakes amongst family members. As we walked back into her living room, I saw the sofa she had died on, and I shuddered. In that split-second, I could see her there, one eye open, a single tear rolling down her cheek. On the edge of the cushion was a little stuffed monkey, a soft toy she'd had for years.

"You're coming home with me, monkey," I said, popping it into my pocket.

Together with Jodey's children, I sifted through her belongings; a favourite dress, a pebble from a day at the beach, a bag she'd bought on holiday. They all had warm and fond memories attached to them. But without Jodey to share them, they felt so hollow. And as I went through her cupboards and drawers, I felt as though I was picking over her bones, ram-raiding her privacy. It didn't seem right. Yet I knew it had to be done.

"Look at this," I said to Jamie, unfolding a paper. "Here's a shopping list of stuff she needed. She never got it because she had no money. All she wanted was washing powder, bread and a magazine. But it was asking too much."

"Oh, Mam," Jamie said. "No point in worrying about that just now. Come and look at these photos with me."

She had plonked a big box of Jodey's photographs on the dining table and, as we searched through, some pictures quickly awakened memories of a birthday party or a family get-together. But with some of the photos, I had no idea where or when they were taken; I had forgotten the time and the occasion. I wished so much that I had paid more attention and noted these things down. Of course, I could never have dreamed how precious a few snapshots would become, how they would be all I had left of my daughter. I stared at the photographs, at Jodey's smiling face, at the changes in her hair style, colour, make-up and fashion, over the years. I wished more than anything that I could reach in and pluck her out of the photos and into my arms.

"Come back, pet," I whispered. "Please come back."

I chose a handful of pictures for myself, along with Jodey's watch and a blue and pink bracelet. Neither was worth anything much, but she had worn them all the time, and so their value, for me, went way beyond money. I picked out three of her handbags too; one black, one red, one pink with a gold chain. She'd always been a magnet for handbags, they were part of her fixation with glamour, but again they were cheap and plastic and probably worthless. Yet to me, they meant the world. I chose a cream jumper that she liked to wear. I could still see her in it and the colour suited her well. And, perhaps most important of all, I took a pink can of Right Guard deodorant. Just one spray reminded me so much of Jodey, it took me right back into her living room, watching *Call The Midwife*, as she pinched chips off my plate. For me, that smell was Jodey.

Eventually, all her possessions were divided up. Some items, inevitably, had to be thrown away. The sofa was on that list. Imagining my daughter's belongings dumped on a scrapheap somewhere was harrowing, and yet it was also a damning metaphor for the way she had been abandoned by the very system which was supposed to care for her. As evening came, I wiped down the kitchen surfaces and hoovered round the carpets, one last time. Jodey would not have wanted to leave the place in a mess.

"There we go, pet," I said, as I wound the cord back around the hoover. "All done, ship shape and sparkly clean."

I had one last look around the flat, now bare and echoey, with all signs of Jodey erased. All that remained were a few marks on the walls where she'd hung her photos and a faint stain on the carpet where she'd spilled a bottle of medicine months earlier. It was unspeakably sad, seeing her life reduced to a pile of cardboard boxes and carrier bags. Jodey, and all her belongings, had been snuffed out. Cancelled. Probably by tomorrow this flat would have new tenants and new dramas and Jodey would be forgotten. It felt appallingly cruel. Like never before, I was struck by how temporary life is.

As we walked down the corridor, I clutched her jumper to me, and I drank in her scent. I was desperate to keep a part of her with me. But as I handed in the keys to the concierge, I was hit by a tidal wave of grief, so powerful it almost knocked me from my feet.

"Are you OK?" he asked, as I stumbled a little.

I nodded, uncertain, and gulped in some air at the front doors.

"She's gone," was all I could manage. "My Jodey is gone."

# 10
# Flicker Of Hope

By the beginning of May, I had still heard nothing from the DWP, and so I phoned to ask for a response to my complaint. Three days in a row, I called, waiting patiently in a long queue, and was then fobbed off every time.

"Someone will get back to you," I was told.

"I hope so," I replied.

That same week, May 4, it was Donna's birthday. I took a present and flowers for her and then went on to the cemetery to have a chat with Jodey. When I came home, my phone was bleeping with an answerphone message. I pressed play for the voicemail as I took off my coat and shoes, and, as I stood in the hallway, quite abruptly, I stopped dead.

"This is a message for Jodey Whiting," said the caller. "Can you please contact the DWP?"

I sank to my knees, right there in the hall, as though every bone in my body had melted and I was no longer able to stand. My daughter had been dead for almost three months and yet the DWP – the organisation which had failed her so unforgivably – was now leaving messages for her. They had ordered a dead woman to find a job and now they were asking a dead woman to call them back. As if that was not sufficiently brutal, they had called me on Donna's birthday. I knew already that they did not care about me or my daughter. But that seemed not to be enough for them. They were determined to prolong my agony, determined to make me suffer over and over again.

"Well, I've got news for you," I said out loud. "I'm determined too. I'm up for a fight."

I pulled myself up from the floor, with a fire burning inside me, and a deep desire for justice and for change.

In the days before the inquest, set for May 2017, I wrote again to the coroner, and also to my MP, Dr Paul Williams, confirming my opinions on why Jodey had taken her own life. In each letter I stressed the involvement of the DWP. The day before the hearing, I called the *Gazette* again, to make sure their reporter would attend. As I hung up, I could feel Jodey next to me, her hand lightly brushing mine.

*I'll call the Gazette if they don't give your benefits back.*

That last vow had stuck in my head and my resolve had hardened around it, like setting cement. The hearing was taking place at Teesside Coroner's Court at Middlesbrough Town Hall and Jamie had offered to drive me there. I had barely slept the night before, with my dreams punctured by images of Jodey leaning too far out her third-floor window, recklessly waving her arms in the air, and shouting to the traffic way below. And every time I pulled her back, closed the window and drew the curtains, she simply found another window to lean out of instead. It felt inevitable that she would eventually fall from the window and that I could not save her. I heard her shouting my name, over and over, urgently, desperately, in those final lonely hours before her death, and I awoke, exhausted.

*I could not save her. I could not keep her safe.*

And even as I showered and brushed my teeth, I heard again my daughter's voice; pleading, imploring:

*I can't walk. I can't leave the flat. I can't breathe.*

As a little girl, when she was bitten by a dog, or banged her head, or drank cough medicine, I soothed her pain with kisses and cuddles. There was no hardship, no drama, that I could not solve for her. In those early days, I had thought, in my naivety and a rush of maternal euphoria, that my love would always be enough to save her. Then, as a headstrong teenager, when she put herself into the care of social services, our bond had been stretched and frayed, but never broken. Never. And when she came home to me, I had promised never to let her go again. I had held her closer still. All through her illness, all through her pain, her depression, her anxiety, I felt that I could carry her. I felt that together, we were strong. But the DWP was a formidable enemy. The DWP was a creeping and deadly toxin. They had stolen my daughter's soul and they had snapped her spirit. Against the might of the DWP, a mother's love was not enough.

For the inquest, I had chosen a smart blue blouse and black trousers. I peered at my pale face in the bathroom mirror and rubbed a bit of colour into my cheeks. I didn't want to let Jodey down. She had always loved to look good, until those final few weeks, and today I could imagine her turning her nose up at my outfit.

*Boring! Boring! Boring!*

I sat at the kitchen table, statue-still, tea and toast untouched, until I heard Jamie pulling up outside. As I turned my head to look out of the window, I caught sight of a shadow, a shimmer, of silvery strands, catching the early morning sunlight and dancing just at the edge of my eyeline. It was gone as quickly as it had arrived, as fleeting as it was insubstantial.

"Jodey," I whispered.

There was no reply, but I knew for certain it was her. Moments later, I was jolted from my trance by the sound of Jamie beeping his horn in the street.

"Ok?" he asked, as he opened the passenger door.

I nodded and swallowed back a tear. I had felt so close to Jodey, in the kitchen, and it seemed wrong to walk out of the house and leave her presence behind.

"Tough day," Jamie said kindly. "We'll get through it."

He looked as drawn and as distraught as I felt. In my hand, I clutched one of my favourite photos of Jodey; a close-up of her smiling. This was her day and I wanted her to be a part of it. She hated to be left out of anything. And above all, I wanted the coroner and the witnesses to know that she was more than a name and a statistic. I wanted them all to see her face, to hear her story, and to know what we had lost. My nerves were jangling as Jamie parked the car, because however much I wanted to be brave, for Jodey's sake, all thoughts of the inquest had taken me naturally back to the day of her death, and all I could think of was finding her body in the flat, slumped on her second-hand sofa, cold and lonely, with the bandage around her leg. That image was burned onto the back of my brain.

*Come on Mam, pull yourself together. You need to tell them the truth today.*

I knew she was right. Now was not the time to crumble. I opened the car door and it felt as though invisible strings were pulling me up, and propelling me forwards, towards the doors of the coroner's court. And I knew it was Jodey, pushing me along. She was there for me when I needed her most.

\* \* \*

Inside the hearing, we were met by the assistant coroner, Jo Wharton. I noticed, as she introduced herself, that she was wearing smart red high heels shoes, and instantly I heard Jodey's voice:

*'Like those shoes, Mam! Do you?'*

One by one, the coroner went on to introduce us to her staff and to the witnesses for the hearing. But there was nobody there from the DWP.

"Will the DWP be here later on to answer questions?" I asked.

But one of the staff shook his head. I could not believe it. Despite my letters, despite my pleas, they had not been called to appear. For me, this was like having a trial without a defendant. The whole hearing seemed like a waste of time, a complete farce. But I could not be bold enough to say that and so instead, I sat quietly in the court, whilst the evidence was examined. Both of my letters to the coroner were read out:

"I am writing this for the sake of my late daughter Jodey Louise Andrea …Her money was stopped by DWP, she was on ESA, they said she never went for a medical but she had never seen the appointment letter. She had curvature of the spine, a cyst on her brain, had been in hospital with pneumonia and deep depression, could not walk out of her house at all…she was really worried about having money stopped, she cried to me, what could she do, she could not go on. She was on 23 tablets a day. She told me Sunday before she died she felt like doing herself in, at that time the police were there. They offered to take her to Roseberry Park but she said no. I wrote, asked the ESA to reconsider, twice, still no. She did not know which way to turn. I tried my best to support and give her what I could. She was sent the second decision on Feb 25, it was still no, but she was dead by then. It is deeply sad. She said she could take no more. They never offered her a second medical…I found her dead on the settee – the image is with us always. She had nine children, two sets of twins, and was a grandmother of 6. I blame the DWP so please take this into account. I would like to attend the inquest. Thank you so much."

Just hearing the words took me back to that day, the tears flowing down my cheeks and onto the page as my grief poured from me like a dam giving way. My second letter said:

"I wrote a letter to you before…DWP were wrong to stop her money, I do believe she had a lot going on and this hit her hard stopping her money. She was on 23 tablets a day…they said she was fit to work, no way. She cried to me, said 'I can't walk, can't breathe'…I'm heartbroken. Please take this into account – I believe she would be alive today if all that had never happened. They were so wrong. Thank you. I included a photo so that she was not just a name."

Though I was grateful my letters had been read out, it seemed somewhat pointless, because the DWP were not here to be cross-examined or to put their own case forward. Next, the hearing heard statements from the paramedic and the police officer who were called to the scene of Jodey's death. There was also a statement from Jodey's GP outlining her many complex health issues.

I had asked if I could give evidence, and though internally I was howling, on the outside I remained as calm and dignified as I could possibly be. And as the coroner began to speak, I was gripped by a steely resolve. She asked me:

"You believe Jodey was under extra stress over the ESA claim?"

"Yes."

"And you believe that that was a contributing factor in Jodey's death?"

"Yes."

She assured me it would be noted. One of Jodey's children said:

"They knew my Mam off a screen…Because of their wrong choice, we've lost our best friend."

And then I added: "I said to her before she died, never thinking this would happen, I said: 'Don't worry Jodey, we will get it sorted and if not, we'll go to the *Gazette*…

"I'd still do that for her. I'm fighting her cause. I want justice for Jodey."

At the end, the assistant coroner stated that Jodey had had her ESA turned down in the weeks before her death and that we believed this caused her extra stress. But she also said that it was not within the remit of the inquest to investigate or comment upon failings by the DWP.

She said: "I note that there are ongoing discussions with the DWP and you've kindly explained that in your letters but it's not the function of this court to question any decision made by the DWP."

She then ruled that Jodey had taken her own life. There was no blame or criticism made regarding the DWP. There was to be no inquiry even, no investigation, no recommendation. I felt deflated; as though someone had sucked all the air and all the energy from me.

As we left, the coroner wished us luck and said she hoped we'd get closure. The entire hearing had lasted only 37 minutes. It had taken a little over half an hour to dispense with my daughter; her life and her death. It felt like yet another stab in the back. I had built myself up to the inquest, hoping and believing that someone would be held accountable for Jodey's death. Yet the hearing felt like a mere formality, as though her death was an inconvenience, a loose end, to be swept up and swept away. Too late, I realised I had been foolish to put my faith in the system. But it was a mistake I would not make twice. If I was going to fight this, I would have to go it alone.

\* \* \*

Outside the coroner's court, I spoke to Ian Johnson, the reporter from the *Gazette*, and I told him I had already made a formal complaint to the DWP.

"We will never get over losing Jodey, and I blame the DWP for my daughter's death," I said tearfully. "The DWP has blood on their hands."

"We'll do what we can to help," he promised.

The next day, Jodey's story was on the front page of the newspaper, with the headline: 'Blood On Their Hands.'

"At last," I said. "At last, someone is listening."

It was a flicker of hope. From there, Jodey's story was picked up by newspapers right across the country, and then, quite incredibly, across the world. The daily papers in the UK all printed my interview, and it was even published as far away as China. As I read through the reports online, I suddenly burst out laughing. My name, Joy Dove, had been translated, by foreign publications, to Pleasure Dove.

"Pleasure Dove," I giggled, wiping my eyes. "What do you think of that, Jodey?"

Somewhere, in the stillness, I heard laughter, and it was a Jodey laugh. Unmistakeably so.

*Pleasure Dove! That's what we'll call you from now on, Mam.*

After Jodey's story went viral, I was contacted by so many people who themselves had suffered because of mistakes by the DWP. Some, like us, had lost family members and they linked the deaths directly with failings by the department. Others had suffered breakdowns, poor mental health, and suicide attempts. I received so many letters and emails and at first, it was quite overwhelming.

"What shall I do?" I gasped, looking at the stack of correspondence laid out on my kitchen table.

I was struggling to cope with my own windowless grief, barely managing to look after myself and my own family, and I did not feel strong enough, or qualified enough, to take on other people's grievances. My own sadness was, quite simply, all consuming. And yet at the same time, I felt a duty and a responsibility to these people. I had spoken out and I had stuck my head above the parapet. Now that I was involved, and I had made a stance, I could not simply walk away. And so I decided, in my own way, that I would offer what help I could.

In time, I would become a conduit for these tragic stories, passing the families on to disability support charities, or putting them in touch with each other, for solace and advice. In some small respect, it was helpful for me, to know that something good was coming from Jodey's death. And it made me realise too that my fight was more important than ever. Jodey's death was a travesty and a tragedy. But it was not the only one. I owed it to her, and to many others, to make sure this never happened again.

After the inquest concluded, I was advised that I could now have a copy of Jodey's full death certificate.

"You will need to collect it in person, from Stockton-on-Tees Register Office," the assistant at the coroner's office told me.

All at once, with those words, I snapped back in time, over 40 years. I had registered Jodey's birth at Stockton Register Office. She was around a week old, and Eric was working that day, so I took Jodey in the pram, with Donna perched on a pram seat. It had been such a proud day, such a happy moment. Years later, the register office building had been bulldozed and a new one built near to the block where Jodey had lived. Allan and I had been married there. I remembered the way that Jodey had danced and smiled at the party afterwards. We'd had a great time, but the memory was so painful now. I knew I needed her full death certificate, in particular for reference for my complaints against the DWP. But I was not sure I was strong enough to make the trip. The register office was practically next door to the block of flats where Jodey had died. It was the same road; the same bus stop. As I took my seat on the bus, I felt a bubble of resistance rising in my throat. I didn't want to collect her death certificate, I didn't want to read it, yet I also knew I couldn't leave it, unclaimed, at the register office. I felt as though I would be letting her down, somehow, by not seeing this journey through. The bus rumbled to a stop outside Jodey's block of flats, and I could have sworn I heard my phone buzz with a text message:

*'Are you nearly here, Mam? Can't wait to see you! Pick up a blue energy drink for me will you please?'*

I checked my phone, praying for a miracle, but of course there was nothing. It was so harrowing, walking past the flats and walking away from her spirit. And inside the register office, I recalled how, when I had registered Jodey's birth in the old building, we had waited on hard plastic seats and Donna had sat patiently next to me, swinging her short legs. Baby Jodey had grizzled and grumbled in her pram next to us.

"You were a handful, even back then," I smiled to myself.

As I waited my turn, a young mother arrived, pushing a pram, and I held open the swing doors for her as she walked through. I listened to her baby, snuffling and murmuring in contentment, and the sounds were so nostalgic and appealing. I wanted to reach out and grab at my own past and pull it back to me. I wanted my time all over again. This time I would not leave Jodey in the flat alone, I would not leave her to die. I would move heaven and earth to save her. I listened as the baby, a girl, was officially registered and I whispered a silent prayer for her.

"Be safe. Be healthy. Be happy, little one."

\* \* \*

Just one month after the inquest, I got a letter in the post, stamped from Karen Hibbert at the DWP. In it, she apologised for the voicemail, which was left on my phone, after Jodey's death.

"This clearly should never have happened..." she wrote. "My apologies for those aspects of our service that fell below our usual standards."

I threw the paper down in frustration.

"Too late!" I cried out. "Too late!"

It had taken the DWP almost six months to acknowledge that they were wrong. If they had done it earlier – in January perhaps when the mistake was first made – I felt certain that my daughter would not have died. All day, as I went about my housework and my shopping, my resentment festered and bubbled like a boil. If the apology letter had been intended to calm me down, then it had had the reverse effect. I was furious at the complacency, the glibness of the language.

*Those aspects of our service that fell below our usual standards.*

It seemed to me as though the letter was addressing a complaint about an overnight stay in a hotel or a problem with my dry-cleaning. The fact was, my Jodey was dead. A life was lost.

That afternoon, still quietly seething, I called the local newspaper and showed them the letter. And then, I organised a family meeting. Jodey's friend from childhood, Debbie, came along too, and my pal, Jan Scott.

"We can't let them fob us off, the same way they fobbed Jodey off," I said. "I want to fight the DWP all the way. I want people to know what they have done."

Everyone was in full agreement.

"What about a social media campaign and a petition to plead for justice?" Debbie suggested.

I didn't have the first idea about social media, I was a typical technophobic granny. But Debbie immediately offered to help.

"We need a name for our campaign," Debbie said, scrolling through her phone, already creating a new Facebook page.

"Justice for Jodey!" I announced.

It was the same simple slogan that I had used at the inquest, and it summed up everything we wanted. It was perfect. Jan offered her support too. She and I had been pals since our first day at primary school, and we'd been through so much together; teenage heartbreak, pregnancies, divorce. We'd felt we could survive just about anything. But never in my worst nightmares had I imagined she would be supporting me through the death of my child. Jan began teaching me the basics of social media so that I could keep up with the comments and messages on the pages. The story ran in the local newspaper and soon, we were getting messages of support from around the UK and beyond. Creating the campaign gave me a sliver of faith to hang onto. This was of course about fighting for justice for Jodey. But it was also a way of directing and harnessing the energy from my grief. 'Justice For Jodey' made me feel closer to her, as though it had in some way resurrected a part of her spirit. When I posted on the campaign pages, I signed off, each time, with 'Justice For Jodey, Love you, Mam. xxx' and I half convinced myself that I was writing directly to her. I loved giving interviews about her too, telling people what she was like and how much she was missed. This was all about seeking justice. But this was also a way of keeping her alive.

* * *

Each day, after I'd finished my cleaning and shopping, I went down to the cemetery to see Jodey. At first, as I walked through the gravestones, it felt surreal. I could not get used to visiting my daughter in this place, and probably I never would. She did not belong here, she was too young, too vibrant, with too much life left to live.

"If I had one wish," I whispered, as I made my way across the graves. "Just one wish. I'd bring you back, Jode."

Most days, if he was free and not working, Jamie would drive me there and visit the grave with me. Other days, I'd get the bus on my own. Eric had paid for a marble gravestone, which read:

'In loving memory of Jodey Louise Whiting. Died 21st Feb 2017 aged 42 years. Loving daughter, mam and nanna.'

As the weeks went by, I took little gifts and trinkets for her, and her children did the same. One took a baby scan and left it on the grave. Another bought her a McDonald's meal. As well as roses, Jodey loved lilies, and I took her a bunch each weekend.

"Look after these," I told her sternly, as I arranged them in a vase on the white stones. "You know they're not cheap!"

Another day, I brought her a copy of the *Gazette*, with her story on the front.

"I'll leave this here for you," I said. "You can read it when I've gone. They've used a lovely photo of you too. My favourite. Everyone's talking about you, pet."

Once, on my way home from the shops, I called in at a café and bought two polystyrene cups of tea. I took them both to the cemetery.

"One each," I said, settling myself down comfortably on the grass with my shopping bags. "Blow on it mind, it's a bit hot."

I wanted so much to believe that Jodey could hear me. I clung to that faith. It was all I had. Each day I spent hours with her, chatting away, keeping her up to date with all the news in the family, and the gossip from her favourite telly shows.

"You would not have believed it!" I'd say, throwing my hands in the air with a smile. "It was so funny!"

And for a moment, just for a split-second, I'd find myself starting to laugh, as though we were sharing a joke together, right there in the cemetery. As if Jodey was listening and giggling, half-way up a nearby tree or hiding behind a headstone. For no more than a moment, it was just like the old times. When I realised my mistake, the feelings of sadness and despair rushed in and clouded my brain like a thick, soupy, fog. My grief felt so heavy, as though it might crush me to pieces.

One night, it was growing dark when I felt an inexplicable urge to visit the cemetery. I had the feeling that Jodey needed me. Usually, I only went to her grave during daylight, but I wrapped myself up warm and got a bus. As I walked through the paths, to find Jodey, I sensed an uneasiness gathering around me, like a cold cloak. Through the gloom, I saw the outstretched arms of marble statues, silent and sinister.

"Jodey," I croaked softly. "Where are you, love?"

It was such a relief when I came to her grave, as though I had found a place of safety and solace.

"I don't like thinking of you here in the dark on your own," I fretted. "It doesn't seem right."

I thought back to Jodey, aged 10, watching *Ghostbusters* in the cinema. She had taken the film so seriously that afterwards, she became afraid of the dark. For weeks, she slept in the same bed as Donna, top to toe, or sometimes she would slip in alongside me. We had to have the landing light on all night too. Thinking of her now, alone in the dark, was unbearable.

"I'm here for you, pet," I told her. "I'm keeping the light on for you at home. Don't be scared."

When it was time to leave, I had to drag myself away. Each time I left her, it felt as though I was leaving a small piece of myself behind, and so it seemed, as time passed, that my grief got worse, not better. And that night when I got home, despite the reassurance of the landing light, I didn't sleep at all. How could I enjoy a nice warm bed, in a safe home, when my own daughter was out there in the cold and the dark? It felt so cruel and pitiless.

"Jodey," I sobbed, with my face in my pillow. "I miss you so much."

The following day, I felt desolate. Trapped in my own despair, I could see no light and no hope and I found myself wandering, almost on autopilot, into my local church, St Joseph's. It was peaceful there, and very quiet. This was the church where Jodey had made her first communion as a seven-year-old. And as I stared at the altar, I could see her, in a white sleeveless dress with a lacy collar and a shoulder length veil covering her chin length wavy hair. Her hands were joined in prayer, eyes reverently down, but, eagle-eyed, I spotted the trace of a smile playing around her mouth. I had tried to catch her eye with a firm look, to remind her to be good in church, but she didn't look my way. Jodey's behaviour was so unpredictable, and I had been on tenterhooks all through the service, worrying that she might lose concentration and start to chat, or even throw a tantrum halfway down the church aisle. Anything was possible! But I needn't have worried. She loved the whole service, she adored the reverence and the honour of the sacrament, and her behaviour was perfect. The memories flooded in and made me smile. Now, I had her communion photo hanging on my living room wall, behind my sofa. And on the sofa cushion sat the little monkey which had once belonged to her.

"You were a good girl really," I whispered. "Most of the time, anyway."

A few days later, I went into the church again and soon I began to look forward to the time I spent there. I began going each Thursday afternoon. It was almost like time off, like a break from my grief and my pain. Sitting there quietly, with my thoughts and my memories, I found such solace. At each visit, I always lit a candle for my daughter. And one afternoon, as I was crying quietly, in the pew, the priest came to sit with me.

"What's troubling you?" he asked.

He was so kind and patient that I had no hesitation in telling him all about Jodey. He listened and then he brought out his Bible and read out loud the most beautiful verse about loss:

"He will wipe away every tear from their eyes, and death shall be no more, neither shall there be mourning, nor crying, nor pain anymore, for the former things have passed away."

I felt certain, in that moment, that Jodey had gone to a better place. Whilst I was in church, my faith was so strong.

One Thursday, I had just finished lighting a candle for Jodey and I was kneeling in a pew, choking back my tears with my eyes closed tightly. Then, in the silence, my mobile phone began playing *Bye Bye Baby* by the Bay City Rollers. I gasped in shock and fumbled quickly to switch it off. My main concern was that I might disturb anyone else who was praying. But then, as I sat on the bench, I realised it had to be a sign from Jodey. I had the song on my phone, but I had no idea how it had unexpectedly started to play all by itself. It was lovely to think that she was contacting me, and playing pranks on me too! And that was exactly the type of thing which appealed to Jodey; playing music in church, pushing the boundaries, causing embarrassment and making people laugh.

"You behave yourself," I murmured, with a smile.

I went home feeling strengthened and bolstered by my visit to the church. But late that same night, when I couldn't settle or sleep, I questioned my beliefs angrily. What kind of God would take a mother away from her nine children and her loving family? It was not fair. Nothing about this was fair. I blamed God, I blamed myself. But above all, I blamed the DWP. I was exhausted beyond reason, yet sleep seemed always just out of reach. And even when I managed to doze, it was only in short snatches of rest, and then I dreamed about Jodey, fighting to get out of the grave, her arms and legs windmilling under a tonne of earth. Each time I tried to pull her out, another pile of soil was tipped onto her body, and I lost her again. It was a hopeless task and just seeing her limbs disappear, under the earth, was a ghastly image I knew I would never forget, even when the dream ended. And every time I awoke, just for a couple of seconds, no more, it was as if nothing had changed and I forgot, temporarily, that Jodey was gone. But those few seconds seemed to last so much longer this time. And then, the truth hit me, smashed into me, like a joyriding car. My daughter was dead. Bereft, I began the grieving process all over again. I could not think of a torture worse than this.

My GP referred me for counselling, which was helpful only in some ways. I felt uneasy about burdening my children and grandchildren with my grief; they, after all, had their own to deal with, and so speaking to a stranger outside of my family was a release. But the counselling brought back the memories of when Jodey was young, and I was reminded of the time I'd needed therapy after suffering with chronic OCD. It had been Jodey who took me to the doctor and insisted I asked for help. And though she was just a young teenager, she had visited me each day in hospital, and thanks to the counselling, and the love of my family, I'd started to feel better. Despite the many challenges she faced herself, Jodey was there for others, and she was there for me. She cared deeply. But when she asked for help herself, she was cut loose and kicked aside by the DWP; abandoned by the very organisation dedicated to the welfare of the vulnerable.

# 11
# Straight To The Top

By July, I was still getting nowhere with my complaint against the DWP and so I decided to step matters up and go straight to the top. This time, I addressed my concerns to Emma Haddad, the Director General of the DWP. As I posted my letter, I allowed myself a wry smile. I would never have been so bold in years gone by, but those social niceties, which had mattered so much to me in the past, now no longer even applied. I didn't care whether I was following protocol or if I was making a fool of myself by writing to the big boss. It didn't matter to me what anyone else thought. I just wanted justice.

Later that month, I received a reply, asking if Ms Haddad and her staff could come from London to visit me in Stockton-on-Tees. My jaw dropped as I read and re-read the letter to make sure I hadn't misunderstood. I was still in shock when Donna called me that evening.

"Wow, Mam, that's amazing," she said. "The top dog is coming all the way from London to see you. Well done."

The team at Citizens Advice were impressed too.

"They're finally sitting up and taking notice of you, Joy," they said. "You should be pleased with yourself."

And I was pleased, but now that I had got my way, I was also a little bit anxious too. I wasn't used to dealing with bigwigs. I'd never even met anyone that important, let alone had a meeting with them! I would have to rehearse everything I wanted to say, I decided, until I was word perfect. I'd have to practise my lines in front of the bathroom mirror. Frantically, I grabbed a pad and pen and began scribbling down my ideas, straightaway.

"Bloody pen's run out," I muttered. "Honestly, how am I going to do this? I'm all over the place."

Then, I had a sudden crisis of confidence about where the meeting would take place. There was not enough room in my tiny one-bedroom flat for visitors, and especially not a delegation of officials from London. And besides, I wasn't sure my place would be grand enough. With a critical eye, I looked around at my furniture; well-loved but well-worn, and I wished I'd redecorated, years earlier. It was too late now. My eyes settled on the photo of Jodey, hanging on my wall, and on her lovely stuffed monkey, perched on my settee.

"What am I going to do, Jode?" I asked out loud. "I've got all these posh people coming. I'm gonna need more than a brew and a slice of Battenberg."

In reply, I could have sworn I heard a faint and familiar snigger.

*'Best hide your false teeth, Mam. You know how visitors like to poke around the bathroom. They will be no different.'*

Just hearing her voice diffused my stress and I giggled. Trust Jodey to think about dentures at a time like this.

"Stop it, will you," I protested. "I'm in a panic as it is without you making me worse."

The next day, I had a call from my MP's office, asking for an update about the campaign, and I mentioned that the DWP hierarchy were planning a visit.

"You're very welcome to hold the meeting in my offices here," said my MP, Dr Williams. "It's nothing fancy but there's plenty of space and, of course, we're used to hosting small events."

"Oh thank you," I replied, flooded with relief. "Honestly, you're a lifesaver."

I ended the call and smirked at Jodey's photo.

"See, I can leave my false teeth out wherever I like," I laughed.

Our MP's office was in the local shopping precinct, on the first floor. The day before the meeting, I called the *Gazette*, the BBC, ITV and the local radio, to invite them all along. If the DWP thought they could keep this meeting under wraps, well, they had another thing coming. Above all, I wanted transparency and honesty. On the day itself, Eric came with me, along with Jamie, and my pal, Jan. Jamie even brought along a camcorder to film the whole event. After all, *we* had nothing to hide. I had been told that a representative from the DWP had called at the MP's offices the day before, to ensure that the premises were suitable. In a funny way, that helped to iron out some of my nerves. What if I'd arranged the meeting at my flat? I imagined an inspector poking around my living room, and it made me giggle.

"Perhaps I should have held the meeting at my place after all and left my dentures and my hair rollers out on the coffee table," I whispered to Jodey. "Now that would give them something to moan about."

We arrived at the offices early, and I was waiting and watching out of the window, when a smart white people-carrier pulled up outside. Out stepped Emma Haddad, Colin Stewart, the area director for the DWP, and a secretary. My hands shook as we made the introductions but afterwards, as we took our seats, a calm settled on me. I had taken Jodey's photo and placed it in the middle of the table where we were all sitting. By focusing on her, I found my confidence growing.

Once again, I went over the catastrophic and unforgivable sequence of mistakes which had led, in my opinion, to Jodey's death. And, of course, the blunders did not stop there. The errors were compounded by the DWP sending letters to Jodey after her death and leaving her voicemails. Perhaps most shameful of all, as she lay dead in the morgue, they had written informing her that she was fit to work.

"It's indefensible, all of it," I said.

Ms Haddad and Mr Stewart had no excuses. After all, what could they possibly say? They assured me that lessons would be learned and promised that staff would be retrained. They also apologised to me, but I shook my head very firmly.

"I can't accept your apology," I replied. "Not now and not ever."

The meeting lasted an hour and a half and, as it came to an end, a ripple of relief trickled through me. I was so glad it was over and I felt proud that I had said my part and that I had stood up for my daughter. We said our goodbyes, and impulsively, I leaned over to embrace Ms Haddad. To my astonishment, Mr Stewart stepped in and barred my way, and I had to move back. It was bizarre and I wondered whether he thought I was going to hurt her in some way. It was a ridiculous assumption, if that was the case, given that I was a little old lady, bent double with arthritis and grief, without an aggressive bone in my entire body.

"I was just going to give her a quick hug," I explained. "Even though I can't accept the apology, I do appreciate you coming to see me. I just wanted to express that.

"I know you've come a long way, and I am grateful, despite everything."

There was an embarrassed silence. And perhaps that one single moment, in microcosm, summed up what was wrong with the DWP. There was, I thought to myself, no humanity at all.

\* \* \*

The remainder of that first summer without Jodey dragged slowly and painfully. Each day in August, I was flooded with memories of trips to the beach or of camping holidays or of ice-creams at the park. I thought of Jodey, as a teenager, sunbathing on the grassy verge outside our house, whilst Madonna blared out of her radio cassette player. I smiled as I remembered the great big multi-coloured tent she had erected in her back garden so that the kids could sleep outside. Now, like then, it seemed to rain every day. It was as though the heavens themselves were weeping with me.

"Why don't we go away for a few days?" Donna suggested. "You need a break, Mam. We both do."

A big part of me railed against the idea of a holiday. The thought of us having fun, and leaving Jodey behind in the cemetery, didn't seem right or fair. I couldn't see a time when I'd ever enjoy a holiday again.

"Jodey wouldn't want this," Donna said, reading my mind. "She'd hate to watch you suffer."

I knew Donna was talking sense. I would be more use to my grandchildren, and to the 'Justice For Jodey 'campaign, if I took some time off and brightened up a little, as tough as that was. By now, I was busy planning a complaint to the Independent Case Examiner (ICE) for the next stages of my fight, and it required concentration and focus.

"Just a day or two then," I agreed.

We booked a weekend in Scarborough, at a cheap bed and breakfast. And Donna was right, it was therapeutic, walking along the beach, breathing in the sea air and listening to the seagulls squawking.

"They say every sailor becomes a seagull after he dies," I told Donna. "What do you think happened to our Jodey? Do you think she might come back as a bird? One of those blasted budgies she used to have perhaps?"

We both laughed at the idea. It was a consoling thought, to think that Jodey might be floating around us nearby. One thing was for sure, I couldn't accept that she had simply gone for good. I felt her near me, I heard her voice, I even sensed a phantom hand hovering over my dinner plate sometimes, ready to steal a chip when I wasn't looking. In my dreams, I heard her calling for me, and I even felt her holding my hand. Perhaps it was wishful thinking. Maybe it was a recognised stage of grief. But I could feel my daughter around me. I knew that she was close.

In October 2017, Jodey would have celebrated her 43rd birthday. We all gathered at the graveside late that after-noon, with a birthday cake and balloons. I'd had two heart shaped plaques made for her grave. The first said: 'Happy

Birthday, Jodey.' The second, a smaller one, was inscribed with the words:

'Till we meet again, love from Mam. xxx'

Early in the evening, we let off fireworks and sang *Happy Birthday*. There were brave smiles pushing through amongst the tears, but it was heart-wrenching for us all, especially when we had to say goodbye, and file out of the cemetery, one by one, without her. That night, I sprayed a little of Jodey's Right Guard deodorant onto my pillow so that I could breathe in her scent.

"Happy birthday, pet," I whispered.

The weeks leading up to Christmas 2017 were pierced with yet more painful memories. I recalled in sharp focus our shopping trip, and that bizarre moment when Jodey had said:

*'If anything happens to me, Mam, don't go screaming.'*

Her words boomeranged back to me now and hit me squarely between the eyes. I had screamed more since her death than in my entire life previously, and in some way, I was still screaming now, deep inside. I was still fighting and flailing against the shock of her suicide.

At Christmas, we took gifts and fireworks to the grave. Someone had brought fairy lights for her headstone, and I'd written her a Christmas card. We had ordered new white stones for her too.

"That will spruce the place up a bit," I told her, as I laid a bunch of lilies at the side of the headstone. "Happy Christmas, Jode."

After Jodey died, I had inherited her keyring, and I'd clipped on a small photo of her, along with my own keys. Throughout December, I walked, rather aimlessly, around the streets near my home, looking through windows at twinkling Christmas trees and families gathered together. Jodey's keyring was safe in my hand, my fingers curled tightly around her photo. It was so precious because it was all I had left of her.

"Hold your loved ones close," I murmured, as I peered through the windows. "You never know when they will be taken away."

I couldn't find it in me to celebrate Christmas properly, but instead I bought a small glass ornamental tree and decorated it with photos of Jodey. I had kept the soap she had bought me, engraved with 'Joy', and I dusted that off too and placed it in my Christmas display. On Christmas morning, whilst still in my pyjamas, I sprayed her Right Guard around the living room.

"Get your Christmas jumper on, pet," I said softly. "Time to unwrap the presents."

I curled up on the sofa, inhaling her aroma, with her toy monkey in my arms. With my eyes closed, I could almost convince myself that she was just next door. Just out of sight.

\* \* \*

By March 2018, my complaint to the Independent Case Examiner was finally ready to be submitted. The complaint was accepted and I was then promised a full investigation. I received a letter telling me that the ICE would look at five key areas:

- Citizens Advice sent a letter to the DWP regarding Jodey's health issues on February 15, six days before her death, but the department failed to act on it until March 23.

- Despite being made aware of her death on February 23 using the 'tell us once' system, the DWP issued a claim to Jodey about her Employment Support Allowance claim on February 25.
- The DWP failed to take appropriate action to upgrade their computer systems until March 1.
- The DWP continued to call Jodey's phone and leave her voicemail messages until May, despite knowing of her death.
- The department failed to respond to my letter of April 13, 2017 until June 14, 2017.

Seeing these failings written down in black and white still, even now, had the power to leave me reeling. I could not, would not, ever understand how or why they had treated her so abominably. I was of the mind that Jodey would have received far more support from the RSPCA than the DWP. No animal would be made to suffer as she had.

I was advised that the complaint would take many months to investigate, and I prepared myself for a long wait. In the meantime, I resolved to continue giving interviews to the local media, and campaigning online, to keep Jodey's name alive. I had done lots of newspaper and radio interviews, but nothing, so far, on TV. Then one afternoon, in April 2018, I was out shopping with my granddaughter, Louise, when my mobile phone rang.

"This is the *Victoria Derbyshire Show* on the BBC," said a well-spoken voice. "Is this Mrs Dove?"

I was so taken aback that I dropped my shopping basket, right in the middle of the aisle in Poundstretcher.

"Are you still there?" she asked. "We wondered whether you would like to come on the show tomorrow morning?"

All at once, I found my voice and shrieked:

"Tomorrow! I can't get down to London that fast! And I've nothing to wear!"

But just as quickly, realising what an opportunity this would be for the campaign, I added:

"Of course, I'd love to though. I really would. I'll be there."

The assistant explained that I could go to the BBC studios in Middlesbrough, which would be much nearer to me. She asked me to be there at 8am, arranged for a cab to collect me, and then she rang off. With my stomach doing somersaults, I looked down at my clothes in dismay; my coat suddenly seemed so tatty, and I'd had my shoes for years. Like a woman possessed, I raced out of the shop and into a nearby Debenhams. I flitted round and round the racks of clothes like a bluebottle; unable to concentrate long enough to even try anything on.

"It's no good," I said eventually. "I'll have to wear something from home. I can't see anything nice here."

Then, on the bus journey home, I started fretting about my hair. Normally, I trimmed it myself! I couldn't believe I was going to be on national telly with a DIY hairstyle. I could hear Jodey chortling in the back of my mind.

"You can stop that," I chided. "You're not the one who has to go on TV!"

As soon as I arrived home, I called Donna.

"Mam, this isn't about your outfit or your hair," she soothed. "This is about Jodey. It's a brilliant chance to talk about the campaign and the petition."

She was right, of course. Together, we picked out a pink jumper and black trousers for me to wear, and I chose a silver heart necklace, which reminded me of Jodey.

"You're going to be fine," Donna assured me.

But even so, the following morning, my mouth was dry with jittery anticipation. I couldn't manage any breakfast. Anxious not to be late, I ordered the cab far too early and left home at just after 6am. Once I was inside the studios, a receptionist smiled and said:

"Good morning, Joy. We're really looking forward to having you on the show."

I was so surprised that she recognised me that I forgot to be flustered, for a moment. And everyone there was so kind too. I was given tea and toast to settle my nerves, and at 10am, I was taken into a studio and told to put on a pair of headphones and focus on a black dot on a screen in front of me. I hadn't realised the interview was via a screen and again I began to panic; my hearing wasn't the best and I was worried I might not hear the questions properly. As I fidgeted on the stool, with the headphones clamped around my ears, I had a strong urge to jump down and run off home.

"Do it for Jodey," I said to myself. "Do it for her."

And in the next second, I heard a famous voice, saying:

"Today, we have Joy Dove, the mother of Jodey Whiting with us…"

Without warning, time seemed to lurch onto fast-forward and the interview was over almost as soon as it had begun. In a daze, I took the bus home. Jamie had recorded the show and we watched it together that same evening. There was a photo of Jodey in the corner of the screen, so that my face was next to hers, and it brought a lump to my throat. It was as if she was next to me.

"You did great, Mam," Jamie smiled. "We're all proud of you."

\* \* \*

And it seemed that the publicity had an instant effect because a few days later, I picked up a report on the radio about Jodey. I listened, amazed, as the news reader announced that Esther McVey, Secretary and State for Work and Pensions, had been heckled whilst speaking to the Scottish Parliament. As she gave evidence, she was confronted by an activist, who shouted:

"What about Jodey Whiting, mother of nine, who committed suicide after her ESA was stopped?"

Knowing that there were so many other people on my side, supporting the campaign, was such a boost to me. Together, we were stronger. After the *Victoria Derbyshire Show*, I spoke to several TV media outlets. I was on my local news channel about once a month, so often in fact that I got to know all the production staff.

"You're a professional now," they winked, as I took my seat in the studio. "You'll be reading the news next."

Over and over, in newspapers, on the radio and on the telly, I told my story. And yet, though I knew the words off by heart, the pain never got any easier. There was no sense of acceptance or of healing. The agony of describing Jodey's passing, and the futility of her death, was as raw and tender now as it had been on the day she died. And in addition to the encouragement we received from strangers, we also had to tolerate online trolling, from people who had very little compassion and even less sense. Reading the comments underneath the articles about Jodey made my eyes pop out.

"If you can't get a job don't have nine kids. Why have 9 kids and rely on benefits…"

"With no judgement or disrespect intended, as obviously it's devastating this lady took her own life, you do have to question how (or better, why) she went through 9 pregnancies and deliveries if her spine problem was so debilitating…"

"Her mental health issues must have been at the forefront here as anyone else who had missed an interview would simply get in touch with the dwp and sort it out. To leave a massive family motherless just because there was a glitch with handouts is a incredible overreaction so she was quite clearly a poorly woman. How on earth can this be the dwp's fault?"

"There's probably a lot more to this story. Making and carrying 9 babies is no mean feat, neither is caring for them, especially if you are claiming inability to work because of pain. You don't get to a state of suicidal tendency in a couple of days, and no doubt she would have been given the opportunity to appeal…"

"The people who are dying are making the choice to so do. They are not thinking clearly when they do this. DWP are an easy target, but it really is nothing to do with them."

Pious, patronising and, of course, completely inaccurate. I knew that by reading those comments I could so easily become as twisted and as bitter as they were, and so instead I decided to ignore them. I had more important issues to consider. By now, thanks to the publicity, our petition calling for justice had 50,000 signatures of support.

"This is all promising," I said briskly. "But we still have a long way to go."

I wrote again to my MP and to the Prime Minister, Theresa May, to ask for help. Sadly, we had not received as much support from disability charities as I might have hoped. MIND had backed our petition, but many charities did not, and I was at a loss to understand why. But by now, I was used to hitting brick walls. And by now, I was happy to walk straight through them.

"If they don't want to help us, we'll carry on without them," I said simply.

Heading the campaign had given me renewed energy and focus. There were days, undoubtedly, when I felt engulfed by my grief, when the weight of my sadness threatened to suffocate me completely. But other times, I had a purpose and a stamina which surprised everyone, myself included. I felt as though Jodey was pushing me forwards, taking half of the strain, alongside me. I never felt that I was on my own.

In February 2019, I finally received the report from the ICE. I had notified all my contacts in the media in advance, so that the findings, whatever they were, could be made public immediately. I had gathered the family together too, and as I tore open the envelope, there was a shared intake of breath.

"This is for you, Jodey," I whispered.

The report was long and complicated, and I don't mind admitting that I couldn't fathom much of what it was saying. But in stark letters, and staring back at me from the page, were the words:

"Significant failings in the events leading up to her death."

The report spoke of "service failures" from the DWP after Jodey died, including a letter confirming her benefits had been cut. The department, it said, had repeatedly failed to apologise for its shortcomings. The DWP had failed FIVE times to follow its own safeguarding rules:

- There had been no consideration in carrying out a home visit when assessing Jodey's eligibility in September 2016.
- There was no attempt to telephone her in January 2017 when she missed her assessment, neither was there a safeguarding visit in January 2017.
- The DWP failed to contact Jodey's GP, despite her request for them to do so.
- There was no consideration for her mental health.
- The DWP had also failed to accept Jodey's telephone request for reconsideration of their decision on 10 February 2017.

The report went on:

"It is clear that Jodey was vulnerable, had been suffering from severe mental health issues and had said she was suicidal.

"I find it extremely disappointing that in investigating the complaints (Joy) raised, we have seen that DWP have either failed to investigate, or failed to acknowledge, the extent of events in Jodey's case."

The regulator ordered the DWP to apologise and to make a consolatory payment for £10,000.

The enormity of what I was reading sent me quite dizzy and I had to sit down. I felt the tide of justification rising within me, so powerful that it literally took my breath away. In many ways, this was vindication. The report confirmed and rubber stamped everything that I had been saying for the past two years. Yet there was no celebration and no cause for joy. Each one of those failings represented, to me, a missed opportunity to save Jodey's life. I was not excited or pleased by the report's findings and this was simply a stepping stone in our campaign. This was one battle won and we had a veritable war on our hands. I passed the report to our local newspaper and the next day, the story ran all over the UK. Under the glare of the media, the DWP were all too quick to apologise.

A DWP spokesperson said: "We apologise to Ms Whiting's family for the failings in how we handled her case and the distress this caused them.

"Our thoughts are with them at this difficult time, and we are providing compensation.

"We fully accept the Independent Case Examiner's findings and are reviewing our procedures to ensure this doesn't happen again."

The apology meant nothing to me. I would never accept it, just as I had not accepted the apology from the Director General, Ms Haddad. In my opinion, they were only sorry that the report had been made public. I did not want the payment of £10,000 either, but it landed in my bank account that same week. It was amazing how efficient and how attentive the DWP were, all of a sudden. Angrily, I divided the payment between Jodey's nine children, I didn't want a penny of it.

\* \* \*

This new efficiency from the DWP made me very resentful. They had ignored me and my daughter for many months and heaped misery after misery upon us. Now that the ICE and the media had taken up our cause, the DWP could not act quickly enough. The payment felt like hush money, as though they thought I could be silenced, as though I was a puppet with my mouth zipped up. But for me, this had nothing to do with money. And I was prepared to shout and scream until justice was done.

Just a couple of weeks after the ICE report was published, the office of my MP, Dr Williams, called to say that Jodey's death would be raised in Parliament, during Prime Minister's questions.

"Hear that, Jodey?" I said, as I put the phone down. "You're going to be discussed in the Houses of Commons today!"

That night, I flicked on the local news for an update. There was a short clip of Dr Williams, saying: "Her family are asking for an apology and to make sure that this can never happen again to anyone else. Can the Prime Minister offer this?"

I held my breath.

Mrs May replied: "He's absolutely right to raise this appalling case that took place and our thoughts and sympathies are with Miss Whiting's family at this time.

"As he said, what's been identified is that there were mistakes in handling her case and it's absolutely right that the department has apologised for their failings, and they are providing compensation to the family.

"That, of course, can never bring Miss Whiting back.

"The point he made is that we need to learn from this case and that is why absolutely the department is looking at that case to make sure that we never see these sorts of failings happening again and leading to such a tragic consequence."

She did not in fact apologise, which was disappointing, but in no way surprising to me. I was beginning to understand more and more about how the system worked, and crucially, how it worked against people like me and Jodey.

Following this new wave of publicity, I was contacted by INQUEST, a charity providing expertise on state-related deaths and their investigation. Part of their aim was to improve the whole investigation and inquest process. I'd had no idea that the charity even existed, and I realised how helpful it might have been in the days following Jodey's death and leading up to her inquest.

"If you can offer me support now, I'd be so grateful," I said.

The charity put me in touch with Merry Varney, a partner at Leigh Day solicitors in London. She had been following my campaign too. It hadn't occurred to me that I might be able to take legal action, and less still that I would be able to afford it. But I was touched by how much Merry knew about Jodey and she was clearly genuinely interested in my cause. I applied for legal aid and Merry explained, over a series of phone calls, that we would make an application to have a second inquest hearing for Jodey and that this time, if we were successful, the role of the DWP in her death would hopefully be properly examined.

We had not been represented at the first inquest and I hadn't even been aware that we might have been entitled to publicly funded legal representation. These were all issues which needed to be addressed going forwards. However, we were warned that permission for second inquests was given very rarely, and that we had a battle on our hands.

"I'm up for the fight," I said.

Over the next few months, Merry and her team obtained documents and information from the DWP, much which I had never seen before. Reading through the paperwork was shocking, heart-breaking and infuriating.

In August 2014, Jodey had filled out a form for the DWP and had written: "Most days I want to kill myself. If my doctor doesn't get my pain under control asap I plan 2 kill myself."

The tears flowed fast and hard as I read her words. Jodey's mental state was clearly spelled out, right there, in writing. They knew how ill she was. And yet still, they stopped her benefits.

I also learned that Jodey had been moved, by the DWP, into an 'ESA support group' because of her mental health issues, and this meant that a red flag would appear on their system, when dealing with her, reminding them that they must seek advice from her GP. This was a safeguarding tool, a back-up plan, to make sure that Jodey did not slip under the radar. But in reality, this had been completely disregarded, and she had been pushed under the radar and trampled underfoot.

My solicitor then commissioned a consultant psychiatrist for his independent expert opinion about Jodey.

In his report, he wrote: "Someone as vulnerable as Jodey Whiting would have experienced distress and shock at the withdrawal of her benefits, given her ongoing difficulties, isolation and pain, and her continuing emotional instability.....likely to generate a substantial depressive impact with activation of suicidal ideas and exacerbation of a negative sense of self...

"It is likely that her mental state at the time of her death would have been substantially affected by the reported DWP failings."

Of course, I knew all of this already; I was Jodey's mother. I had watched her daily deterioration after her benefits were withdrawn with a growing sense of alarm and helplessness. But I considered it a big step forward to have my claims confirmed and validated by a consultant psychiatrist. And because none of this evidence had been heard at the first inquest, it was felt that we had a chance of being granted leave to apply for a second inquest.

It was galling to learn of yet more DWP failings in this latest information, but I was determined not to let it drag me down. I needed to look to the future now, to a legal battle, and to justice.

# 12
# Centre Stage

In July 2019, I was contacted by a filmmaker and disabled rights activist named Dolly Sen. She had seen our campaign and wanted to ask if I would take part in a documentary she was planning, along with disabled artist Caroline Cardus, to focus on the failings of the DWP.

"Yes definitely," I replied. "What do you want me to do?"

Dolly was planning a peaceful 'broken hearts' protest outside Caxton House, the London headquarters of the DWP, which aimed to highlight how DWP polices had caused thousands of broken hearts.

"Is that even allowed?" I asked. "Won't we be arrested?"

But even as I spoke, I knew that I would be there, no matter what the risk. In the early morning of July 25, Jamie and I set off to take a train to London. I hadn't been down to the capital since 1983, on a day trip with the kids. It had been such an exciting adventure back then but now it felt overwhelming. Arriving at the station, I was fearful of the bustle and the rush and the noise. The place was cavernous, like a shiny, modern, cathedral. Commuters dashed past me, all crowding towards the platforms, and I felt so out of my depth. If I couldn't cope at the train station, how on earth would I manage to take part in a protest in central London?

"You're doing it for Jodey," I reminded myself.

I took deep, calming breaths and clutched her photo tight in my hand. Even so, I was glad to have Jamie with me. The system of automated ticket barriers and the long digital lists of arrivals and departures was mind-boggling.

At Whitehall, we met with Dolly and her team, and also the families of three other disabled people, Stephen Carre, Mark Wood and Susan Roberts. They had all lost their lives after their benefits were stopped or reduced. Dolly handed us large red placards, in the shape of broken hearts, each with a name on. When I saw Jodey's name, with a split right down the middle of a heart, I broke down.

"How did it come to this?" I wept.

There were other placards at the protest: 'Broken Hearts for the DWP' and 'Hearts stopped by DWP policies.' We all stood in a line, outside the DWP offices, and Dolly spoke over a loudspeaker. I felt many extremes of emotion. And mixed in with my anger, my grief and my pride, was a teeny bit of excitement too. It felt rebellious, shouting out slogans on a London street, clutching my symbolic heart in front of me. It was just the kind of thing Jodey would have loved too, to cause a bit of a fuss and a spectacle in public. I had taken a 'Justice For Jodey' banner with me, and together with Dolly, I stood in front of the DWP doors and held it high. There was a collage of photos on the banner, each taken over the 42 years of her life. Each a memory of a happier day.

Every time a staff member went through the large glass doors, I shouted out:

"Jodey Whiting! Justice For Jodey! You have blood on your hands!"

It was exhilarating; at the age of 65 I had become an activist, a revolutionary! I had visions of me being arrested and dragged away by my ankles, with footage beamed into living rooms on *News at 10*. I pictured the kids back home spotting my face amongst the melee and it made me giggle.

"Justice for Jodey!" I yelled, louder this time.

I didn't expect the DWP staff to reply or even to acknowledge my presence, and of course not one of them did. But I wanted to remind every civil servant and every government minister how the actions of the DWP had a ripple effect which had led to my daughter's death.

Over her loud-speaker, Dolly said: "Joy is here to mourn that her daughter has passed because of this building behind us.

"We want these hearts to be still beating. The more hearts that are stopped by the building behind us, the stronger our hearts will get.

"We will fight for every person who is let down by the building behind us.

"The workers who are going in and out may not have physically killed somebody, but they are the cogs in a system that is churning out coffin after coffin after coffin.

"We want more people to know what's going on. This is a symbolic protest: a heart that goes de-dum, de-dum, de-dum, and it just stops because of this building.

"To me it is just a horrific and really painful thought. If you took this building out of the chain of decisions, people would still be alive."

On the train journey home, I no longer felt intimidated or dispirited. The protest had given me back my confidence and my passion and I couldn't wait for the next stage of Dolly's documentary. Sadly, afterwards, the protest didn't receive much coverage in the media. Apart from an article in *Disability News*, I didn't see any other reports. I couldn't understand at all why this issue was not a national outrage, and why there were not millions protesting on the streets. What kind of society left its weak and its helpless to die alone? And then accepted those deaths without so much as a whimper?

\* \* \*

One of Dolly's team, Paula, was a disability rights activist, and after the broken hearts protest, she had asked me if she could pass my number onto the famous filmmaker, Ken Loach. He was one of my favourite film directors and in 2016, a matter of months before Jodey's death, he had directed the award-winning film *I, Daniel Blake*. In it, the character Daniel is denied ESA despite his doctor confirming he is not fit for work. The film portrayed the very real devastation caused by austerity for so many people, and it was critical too of the mind-boggling bureaucracy of the benefits system. I had watched it more than once and thought it brilliant, but terrifyingly close to the bone for me too.

"Sure," I agreed, when Paula asked, though really, I couldn't for the life of me see why someone like him would want to speak to me.

A few days later though, my phone rang, and a voice announced himself as Ken.

"I was so sorry to read about Jodey," he told me. "I've been following your interviews and your campaign. It breaks my heart. Nothing has changed since *I, Daniel Blake*.

I chatted to Ken for over an hour. He was so down to earth and genuine, and even over the phone, I could feel his warmth and concern. After our phone call, Ken posted on Twitter: "The DWP is still failing people – it may be worse now than it was when we made *I, Daniel Blake*." He had added in a link to my petition calling for an independent inquiry into deaths linked to the DWP. Afterwards, he wrote to me, again backing our campaign and affirming his support.

His letter read: "It has clearly been a hideous situation for you and the whole family – and your courage in pursuing justice for your daughter is humbling.

"We are aware of countless other stories like yours, where the DWP has shown brutality that has led directly to innocent people suffering, and even death, as with Jodey."

\* \* \*

One fine afternoon in August 2019, I was busy tidying Jodey's grave when my phone rang. To my surprise, it was one of the senior writers from the *Daily Mirror*, who'd previously written several stories about Jodey and about our campaign.

"I know this is a big ask," she began. "It's the Labour Party annual conference in a couple of weeks and we wondered whether you would speak at the event, Joy?"

I gulped. Panic coursed through me. But then, I looked at Jodey, smiling back at me from the photos on her grave, and I realised there was only one reply.

"Course I will," I said. "It would be an honour. You know, I'm with Jodey now, as it happens, and I can't help thinking that it's a sign."

She explained that my travel and accommodation would be paid for, and that I could bring one person along with me, for moral support.

"I'll bring Jan, my friend," I said immediately.

The conference was in Brighton in September, and it was arranged that we would travel down by train the night before, and that I would make my speech the following day. At the mention of the word 'speech' I felt a stab of anxiety, as though someone was tying my insides up in knots. And then, of course, there was the eternal question of what I would wear!

"You'd best make an effort, Mam," Donna teased me. "The place will be jam packed with celebs."

That week, I did a whistle-stop tour of all the charity shops in Stockton-on-Tees and found a bargain blouse for £2 and a pair of grey trousers. I could sense Jodey screwing her nose up a little; it was a very sensible and demure outfit and Jodey would definitely have gone for something more colourful and audacious.

"I've got to make a good impression," I reasoned with her. "There will be all sorts of famous faces there."

Eric had offered to drive Jan and I to Darlington train station and, on the morning of our trip, I asked if we could set off a little early so that I could stop by at the cemetery and have a chat with Jodey.

"I just want to talk it through with you," I said, as I sat by the gravestone. "I need to make sure I'm doing the right thing for you."

As I spoke, my mind was suddenly crowded with last-minute doubts. I remembered the online trolls, and those people who hadn't been supportive, and I worried I might be putting myself – and Jodey – in the firing line.

"I'm proud of you, Mam," came a whisper through the trees. "This isn't just for me, it's for everyone who was failed by the DWP. You need to speak out."

"Thanks pet," I replied. "You're talking sense."

I left the graveside filled with a strong sense of purpose and resolution. I had with me my good luck charm; my keyring, with Jodey's photo hanging from it. Eric dropped us at the station, for our train to King's Cross, London. It was a two-and-a-half-hour journey and I had planned to use the time to work on my speech for the conference. I had brought a notepad and pen, but, as the train whizzed past housing estates and industrial units, fields and reservoirs, my mind was unexpectedly blank. The magnitude of the occasion was weighing heavy on me now, this was the Labour Party conference after all, and the clarity I had felt, hours earlier at the grave, seemed to slip through my fingers like sand. I kept on crossing ideas out and adding them back in. Each time I read it through, I made more changes. I had brought egg sandwiches and snacks for the train, but I was so engrossed in writing my speech that I forgot all about them. We pulled into King's Cross, and I packed my things away quickly, ready for the next change. Minutes later we were dashing across the platform to jump on the Brighton train – and just in time too. As we settled into our seats, and the train gathered pace, there was an announcement from the conductor: "Welcome aboard this train to Gatwick Airport."

"Gatwick!" I shrieked, jumping up out of my seat. "But we're going to Brighton!"

In our hurry to make the train, we had taken the wrong connection. Thankfully, a helpful guard explained we could still get a Brighton train from Gatwick, so all was not lost. And when we arrived at Gatwick, he kindly guided us onto the correct train.

"Honestly, I can't even get on the right train, and I'm supposed to be giving a speech to Jeremy Corbyn tomorrow!" I gasped.

The entire journey took us over six hours, because of the detour, and we were thoroughly exhausted by the time we arrived at the Brighton Travelodge. As we signed in, the receptionist peered at our names and said:

"Oh, you're with the Labour Party conference, aren't you?"

"I am indeed," I smiled, feeling myself grow at least another inch.

As I mentioned at the start of this book, I was very nervous before I gave my speech to the conference. But as I stood there holding photos of Jodey, I found the confidence to go on, telling the delegates that I'd never give up my fight for justice.

* * *

As the applause died down, I sank into a chair, flushed with relief. Afterwards, I was guided back through the foyer and into a huge reception room with a lavish buffet and drinks laid out. It was surreal watching the other guests file in; Kevin Maguire, the associate editor of the *Mirror*, was there, as were Ken Livingstone and Jeremy Corbyn. I felt as though I'd stepped into a parallel universe.

"I just need some air," I said, wafting my face with a napkin. "I won't be a moment."

It felt good to have the sea air pinch my cheeks and remind me that the world outside was still turning, just the same. I had a quick walk up and down the promenade, and, as I was preparing to go back into The Grand, I spotted an elderly man lingering on the pavement. From his clothes, and his manner, I guessed he might be homeless. At the very least, he looked in need of a square meal.

"Come in here and have some of this buffet," I said to him. "Honestly, you won't believe the spread. There's plenty to go round."

We waited with security whilst I got clearance from the conference staff, and then he came inside to sit beside me. I smiled as he piled his plate high. I thought about the egg butties, still mulching in the bottom of my handbag, and I stifled a giggle.

"This is a step up from my cooking," I said to the old man. "We should make the most of it."

All that afternoon, I was introduced to various celebrities and activists, all of whom pledged their support for Justice For Jodey. It was humbling to know how far − and how high − our campaign was reaching.

"You'd have loved this, Jodey," I whispered softly.

*"I'm here, Mam, I'm counting the chocolate eclairs you're eating, don't you worry!"*

Just inside my eyeline, I spotted a well-dressed woman with a large handbag; fluorescent pink with gold tassels and fancy gold straps.

*"Ooh, I love that. Just my style. Can you have a word with her, Mam, see where she got it?"*

The reception came to an end, and afterwards I listened, enraptured, to another round of speeches. Then, it was back to the Travelodge to pack our things ready for our train the next morning. But I wasn't ready to leave. I loved telling people about Jodey, and it was cathartic to describe how special she was and how much we missed her.

"I'd stay the whole week if I could," I said to Jan. "I'd quite like to be a politician, especially with all those free cakes!"

Early the next morning, we had a quick sausage butty at the hotel before we left for the station. But by the time we were pulled in at King's Cross, we were both feeling peckish again, and, with time to spare until our next train, I nipped into a nearby Tesco Express. To my delight I managed to find a pack of chocolate muffins and a pack of apple pies, both on the reduced shelf.

"Look, cut price, only a pound each," I announced triumphantly, as I found Jan waiting on the station concourse.

We still had time to kill and so we found a cafe for a coffee, and then went to board our train. As the journey got underway, I rummaged around for the cakes and realised I had lost them.

"I think I left the shopping bag at King's Cross," I groaned. "I could murder an apple pie. Jan, I really could. They weren't such bargains after all."

"The bomb squad is probably detonating your chocolate muffins right now," Jan winked. "You're a security risk!"

I clapped my hands over my mouth and gasped. She had a good point. Luckily, there were no reports of suspicious packages and we arrived home safely, late that night, dropping with exhaustion but puffed out with pride. My speech was widely reported in the media, and I hoped that Jodey's story might reach other families and other vulnerable people. I hoped that maybe, just maybe, it might even save a life.

# 13
# Fuel To The Fire

When the lockdown of spring of 2020 came, the cemeteries were closed, and I was no longer able to visit Jodey's grave each day. It tore me apart, thinking of her all alone, inside the graveyard, asking herself why she had been abandoned. Outside my window, the spring flowers pushed through, but they reminded me sharply of Jodey and of the daffodils we had placed in her coffin. I resented these green shoots of new life when my daughter's life, and my own, were forever stuck in February 2017. I missed her terribly and I knew I could not cope without my daily visits to the grave. And so instead, I built a little shrine in my flat, with photos and five candles spelling out the letters of her name. I included Christmas and Mother's Day cards and my favourite photos and the final few gifts she had bought for me, including my precious soap. I added in a packet of her favourite Rainbow drops and an energy drink too. I even allowed myself a quick burst of her Right Guard, and the smell was so uniquely Jodey that I turned around sharply, almost expecting to see her there. Afterwards, crushed by my disappointment, I sank back on the sofa, closed my eyes, and inhaled her clean, crisp smell. I could have sworn that Jodey was sitting right next to me, helping herself to the Rainbow Drops whilst I wasn't looking.

Still, she figured in many of my dreams, and in many different forms. In one recurring sequence, I caught only a fleeting glance of her, and she appeared wraith-like and insubstantial, as though she was nothing more than a mirage. Her clothes swirled around her in a fog, and when I tried to reach out and touch her, she dissolved and shattered into tiny pieces. When I awoke, I was pinned to the bed with immobilising grief, as numbing as it had been on the day she died.

In other dreams, Jodey was laughing and carefree, with her disabilities and her pain miraculously cured. She wore bright clothes in vivid colours, as though she was off to a party, and I noticed in dreamy amusement that she was carrying the pink handbag from the Labour Party conference.

"Come home," I urged her. "Come back to us, Jodey."

But still smiling, she skipped away.

"I can't afford to come back," she replied. "I was a burden on Earth. But here, I am free."

It was unbearable, even in a dream, to watch as she disappeared, out of sight. And when I awoke, I felt cheated, I felt violated. These passing glimpses of my daughter, and the crushing realisation each time I woke that they were not real or permanent, only served to make my heart ache even more.

"Why?" I asked, over and over. "Why Jode?"

One afternoon in April, I nipped out to buy milk, and, as the first drops of rain began to fall, I opened my umbrella. At that moment, a bee flew under my brolly, and I shrieked in panic. I had always been terrified of bees, ever since I was a little girl. As it buzzed towards my face

I stumbled awkwardly to the side and a shooting pain tore through my back like a jolt of electricity. My eyes watered with pain as I stood in the middle of the pavement, unable to move. The bee thankfully disappeared, and my brolly lay upended on the ground. Somehow, grimacing with each small movement, I managed to call Jamie, and he came to my rescue immediately to drive me home.

"You shouldn't be out in lockdown, it's risky at your age," he told me sternly. "Let's get you safely inside."

I was sure it was just a slight strain, but the next day, my back was in agony again. I called the GP and was referred for an X-ray but was warned, with the Covid delays, it might take some time. Instead, I bought myself a walking stick and soon I was relying heavily on painkillers. Jamie drove me every-where, and though I did my best to help him out with his fuel bills, it was such a struggle. I was in debt myself, behind with my council tax payments and the repayment of a social fund loan. The comparisons were not lost on me; this was a mere snapshot of the misery and desperation that Jodey must have felt, constantly juggling pain and worry and debt. Often, I was in too much discomfort to sleep at night, and I felt closest to her then. I even typed out a text message to her:

"U awake? Can't sleep. Back driving me mad."

*"I am now, Mam! Honestly!"*

Over the weeks, the pain ground me down, eroding my usually positive outlook. My back would stiffen so that I couldn't move at all and the pain radiated to every part of my body, until even blinking felt like an effort. For 10 days, I remained propped up on the sofa, barely sleeping, barely existing. Again, the analogy with Jodey's situation was unavoidable.

"Jodey lived with this pain, and much worse, for years and years," I said sadly to Donna. "She was so brave. I don't know how she stuck it for as long as she did."

* * *

Jodey's nine children had all suffered dreadfully since her death. In their own individual ways, they grieved, and they stumbled on. The catastrophic ramifications of her passing touched not only her children, but their partners, her grandchildren, her nieces and nephews. But Cory, just as Jodey had predicted in those letters written before her death, seemed to struggle the most. I'd heard disturbing tales, from his older siblings, about him sleeping on his mother's grave at night. Other times, he'd sofa-surf around his family and friends. He seemed to have lost all direction, and with it, hope.

By 2020, aged 19, Cory was leading a chaotic lifestyle. I wanted so much to help him, but I couldn't get through to him, and most of the time, I didn't even know where he was. I saw him in April 2020, but he seemed distant and preoccupied.

"It's tough without your mam," I sympathised. "I know that."

He nodded uneasily in reply.

One morning, the following month, Louise called, and I sensed, before she even spoke, that my heart was about to be ripped apart yet again.

"It's Cory," she sobbed. "He's gone."

He had been found dead from an overdose. Still only a teenager, his life was over before it had barely begun. Jodey's words in that final letter swam around my head:

'I hope sum 1 will love my twins…Cory is gonna end up dead…I av 2 go 2 b waiting 4 him. God forbid tho.'

Just as she had predicted my screaming, she had predicted her son's death. The prophesy was testament to the bond that Jodey shared with her children because she knew that Cory would not cope without her. Of them all, he was the most fragile, and he needed her the most. The confirmation of that bond only served to make her death yet more painful and I held the DWP responsible now for his death, as well as hers. And though my heart was bruised and battered, his death added fuel to the fire and the fight that burned inside me.

\* \* \*

In September, I travelled down to London to film the next part of the documentary with Dolly. This time, Donna came along with me.

"We'd better make sure you don't leave your bags any-where or get on the wrong train," she teased. "We know what you're like."

By now, I knew Dolly well and I was looking forward to the reunion. I had kept in touch with the other families too, and it brought me such solace to talk to them and to know that, however desperate we might feel, we were not alone. The families couldn't all meet in person this time, because of lockdown rules, and instead we chatted online.

I was interviewed by Dolly about Jodey and when I got to the part where I found her body, the shock hit me afresh, like a rolling breaker. Each detail was as clear to me now as it had been on that tragic February evening.

It was October 2020 by the time the X-ray results for my back were processed and, to my astonishment, the doctor revealed that I had three fractures in my spine, due to osteoporosis.

"No wonder you've been in agony, Joy," he said.

I was prescribed more medication and stronger painkillers, but my new tablets made me sickly and nauseous. Again, I thought of Jodey and all those years of trial-and-error combinations of her 23 different tablets. How had she coped with that? I went back to hospital for an MRI scan and after the procedure, my body seized up completely. It took two nurses to lift me out of the MRI machine and off the stretcher, and I screamed in agony every time they touched me. Again, my thoughts were pinned very firmly on my daughter. This was just a small slice of what she had endured. How could anyone ever have thought that she was fit to work?

The following month, my solicitor, Merry Varney, applied to the High Court asking for leave to appeal for a new inquest into Jodey's death. It was more than three years since the start of our campaign, and my legal fight had finally begun in earnest. I was told we might wait up to six weeks for the decision to be made. But just three days on, as I pottered about at home, I got a call from Merry.

"We've got it!" she announced. "We have leave to appeal."

It was brilliant news. I gripped the phone, and I wanted to reply, to thank her, to tell her how thrilled I was. But I couldn't speak because tears were pouring down my cheeks. I missed Jodey more than ever in that moment. I wanted her with me, to celebrate. I wanted her to see how far we had come.

Our application for the new inquest was formally submitted in December 2020 at the High Court in London.

The news was reported in the national media, and I was then contacted by a second documentary company. I agreed immediately, of course, to take part in filming. The way I saw it, each piece of publicity, each story, each film, had the potential to save a life.

"I want Jodey Whiting to become a household name," I said. "The system will change, because of her."

Through the publicity, and also through Justice For Jodey, I continued to hear from dozens of families who had been affected by failings in the DWP. Tragically, some families had lost a loved one, like me. Others, claimants themselves, had been affected mentally and physically by a reduction or a removal of their benefits. I felt as though I was amassing an army; one by one, people were joining in and helping our cause. It had started off as a solitary and lonely journey but now I felt part of a huge groundswell, a revolutionary movement that was gathering pace daily. There was strength in numbers and strength in love.

I'd find myself on the phone until late at night easing complete strangers through stages of their mourning. Many of them I had never met, and would never meet, and yet we had a unique and tragic bond which bound us together.

Mostly, I took heart from offering my support. My own loss helped me to help others; it gave me a purpose and it gave Jodey a legacy. I encouraged everyone I spoke with to make formal complaints and to push for legal action and public accountability.

"This is the only way that we can push for change," I told them.

There were days when I felt crushed by my own grief, when I felt cowed and broken by my own situation and I could not see past the loss of my own daughter. On those occasions, my friend, Jan, or maybe Donna or Jamie, would step in and take over at the campaign hub, whilst I recharged my emotional batteries.

* * *

Christmas 2020 was our fourth without Jodey and I felt her loss as keenly as ever. Early on Christmas morning, as other families swapped gifts and hugs, I made my way to the cemetery with a card and a bunch of lilies.

"Where are you, Jodey?" I asked helplessly. "Send me a sign, pet. Anything at all."

I looked up to the skies and searched for her face in the low ribbon of grey cloud. But there was nothing. The distance stretched between us, a screaming chasm of loss, so loud, it drowned out my own voice and the sound of the city around me.

The warmth of the spring sunshine in May 2021 brought with it promising news from my solicitor, and I hurried straight down to the cemetery to share the update with Jodey.

"Our hearing is scheduled at the High Court in London for June!" I said excitedly, as I pulled out a few rogue weeds from around her grave. "Can you believe it, pet? You're taking on the whole of the establishment!

"Who would ever have thought it!"

I had taken the solicitor's letter with me, so that I could read it to her word for word.

"Our Jamie says he will come with me. The documentary team are coming too, they will be filming me outside the courts. I'll have to make sure I look the part."

I would have liked to have stayed longer at the grave, it was a bright day and there were geraniums budding around the headstone. Normally, I loved spending time with Jodey. But today my backache was so bad, I could hardly bear it.

"I'll have to go, Jode," I said. "I'm sorry. My back's playing up again. I need to get home for my painkillers. I have no clue how you put up with all that agony for so long. I really don't."

I hobbled off to the bus stop, taking each tentative footstep through gritted teeth. I had no idea how I was going to make it to London in this state. But I also knew that nothing in the world would stop me.

# 14
# Taking On The Establishment

In early June, my solicitor called again to say that, only 10 days before our hearing date, the DWP had asked for permission to make legal arguments relating to our application.

"Why would they do this now?" I asked, my hackles rising. "They have known about the hearing since December. Why do this to me at the last possible minute?"

I was constantly insisting that nothing the DWP did could shock me anymore, yet I was appalled by this latest development. The DWP had shown callous disregard for the anguish they'd caused Jodey during her lifetime and now they seemed intent on causing me yet more distress. I had been working myself up to facing the hearing for weeks, and this felt like yet another attempt to upset and unsettle me. Yet another blow. I didn't understand it; this was not a time to employ tactics. I was not the enemy here; I was the victim. Or perhaps Jodey and I were so unimportant, so insignificant, that the DWP were only just getting around to considering our legal challenge, a few days before it was scheduled to take place. Maybe I hadn't even figured in their plans, until now. I could feel my anxiety growing, but I took deep breaths and reminded myself that nothing could be as bad as losing Jodey. After that, I could cope with anything they threw at me. Anything at all. But then my solicitor explained that the DWP's last-minute request might even delay the date of the hearing until later in the summer. It was annoying and it was inconsiderate, but there was nothing I could do. I was totally helpless, following the developments from home, through online news and updates from my solicitor.

Jesse Nicholls, from my legal team, told the high court that the DWP had known about our bid for a new inquest back in December 2020, but had only applied to be part of the case on June 2.

He said: "The idea that the (DWP) would make an application at such a late stage without explanation and that would put the hearing back would cause great distress."

Jonathan Dixey, for the DWP, said the department regretted the delay and would "self-limit" its arguments to make sure the case was not delayed.

"The Secretary of State has a proper interest in the proceedings themselves. It is said as a result of the DWP's acts or omissions, Ms Whiting took her own life," he said.

The judge, Mr Justice Morris, ruled the DWP could make written arguments at the High Court hearing.

He said: "I am very conscious of the extremely distressing background to this case… the distress it must have caused Ms Dove and continues to cause."

Mr Justice Morris then decided it was in the public interest for the DWP to make arguments, adding they may be a part of the second inquest if it goes ahead. But to my relief, he said the hearing on June 22 would not be moved, but would spill over into a second day, and the DWP would have to pay 30% of my costs for the hearing.

"It seems to me that the Secretary of State has come to this court asking for an indulgence very late in the day," Mr Justice Morris concluded.

The judge added that, while the DWP regretted the delay, "this fell somewhat short of an explanation or an apology".

He said: "It is suggested that this is a matter of great importance to the DWP. If this is the case, it begs the question that if it was so important, why did the DWP completely fail to make an application to participate?"

I raised a wry eyebrow as I read his comments. The DWP made lots of mistakes. This was just one in a very long line of errors.

\* \* \*

The day before the June hearing, Jamie and I took the train down to London. We were booked in at a Premier Inn, for two nights. Despite my painkillers, I was in a lot of discomfort. I needed my walking stick, even for short distances, and with support I could only move very slowly and with frequent rests. It was a nuisance, especially in a fast-moving, bustling city like London. Yet it appeared to me somehow fatalistic that I was crippled with back pain, before the hearing, as though this was representative of Jodey, and of all the disabled people who had been swept aside and let down by the DWP's system. Her pain was in some way embodied through my own, and the walking stick, whilst it was primarily an aid, became an emblem for Jodey too. I had her with me, on my keyring, as always.

I had brought her photograph, and my Justice For Jodey banners. And more than that, she was in my heart.

On the morning of the hearing, Jamie and I left the hotel early. I had been up since 5am, unable to sleep a wink. By the time Jamie woke up, I was already waiting, dressed in smart black trousers, a white blouse and a dark grey jacket. I was a little more used to these occasions by now and certainly didn't stress over my outfits the way that I once had.

"Alright, Mam?" he smiled, giving me his arm.

There were two camera crews and a pack of reporters waiting for us as we approached the High Court. I was over-awed by The Strand itself, even before we had arrived at the court itself. Each building was breath-takingly beautiful, this was architecture and opulence from a bygone age. I could feel it in the air, the sense of occasion, the magnitude of our mission, and it felt almost religious. Before we spoke to the press, I posed for a quick photo under the sign: 'The Royal Courts of Justice.'

"Wait till I show the kids," I smiled.

Outside the courts, I met my solicitor, Merry, for the first time. We had often chatted on the phone and over Zoom but this was our first in-person meeting and we hugged like old friends.

"You look very smart," she said approvingly.

"Charity shop bargains," I winked. "Can't beat 'em."

Once inside the great foyer, I was struck immediately by the rarefied and reverent atmosphere, by the dark panelled walls and the lofty ceilings. There was even a line of mannequins, dressed in judges' costumes, each from a different era. This was like stepping straight into a period drama. And it was as far away from Jodey's North East tower block as you could possibly get. We all waited patiently in line to have our bags searched and when it was my turn, I reached into my pocket to dutifully hand over my phone.

"No phone!" I gasped, patting my other pocket, and then rummaging frantically around my handbag. "I've lost my phone!"

I groaned as I remembered nipping into Pret A Manger on my way, to use the loo, and placing my phone on top of the hand-dryer, whilst I was washing my hands. Only now, did I realise my mistake.

"It's in the ladies' loos!" I announced. "I'll have to make a dash back for it."

"There's no time," Merry said, checking her watch. "The hearing starts in less than 10 minutes."

Instead, her assistant, Dan, helpfully offered to sprint back to the coffee shop to see if he could find it. As we passed through security, one of the barristers for the DWP walked past and accidentally dropped one of his books. Instinctively, I picked it up and hurried after him, before handing it back. I felt my back cracking as I straightened up, but I managed to groan only inwardly. He looked somewhat nonplussed but nodded his thanks.

"You do realise that was the barrister for the opposition," Jamie said to me, shaking his head.

"Yes of course," I replied. "But it doesn't cost anything to be kind or courteous. That's a lesson we can all learn, especially the DWP."

Outside the door to the court, I spotted a sign which said: 'Joy Dove v Secretary of State.'

The notice sent a curious rush of both panic and pride through me. Who on earth was I to take on the establishment like this? What the hell was I thinking? I was a little old lady, and surely, I was supposed to be at home with a brew and a digestive watching daytime telly! Yet, in the very next thought: Why the hell shouldn't I be here? If not me, then who else?

*Blow the digestive biscuits, get ready for the fight, Mam! All the way from Benefits Street to the Royal Courts of Justice!*

I thought of Jodey, I thought of all the families who I'd met through the campaign, I sucked in a deep breath which felt as though it filtered right down to my toes, and I marched into the courtroom with my head held high. We were just taking our seats when Dan joined me, slightly breathless.

"Good news and bad news," he whispered. "They have your phone, but they won't give it to me because it has your bus pass in the back with your photo on! You will have to go back and collect it during the lunch break."

I whispered my thanks and stifled a giggle.

*'Typical, Mam! You leave your chocolate muffins at the train station and now you leave your phone in the coffee shop! You're a one-woman walking disaster!'*

Moments later, a clerk instructed us all to stand and then bow, as three judges – Lord Justice Warby, Mrs Justice Farbey and Judge Thomas Teague QC, the chief coroner for England and Wales – swept majestically past us and took their places. I had been warned not to speak at all, but I found I had to physically clamp my lips together to stop myself from making comment. In my mind, I was oohing and aahing and drinking in the little details of the scene, so that I could later describe it to Donna.

*'Oh, Donna, you should have seen their wigs! Honestly, the place was dripping with wealth! I bet one of those paintings is worth more than my flat!'*

The Secretary of State, as well as members of the media, were in attendance over Zoom. Hours into the proceedings, my concentration drifted. I wanted so much to keep up, but I got lost in the legal jargon of the argument and counterargument. Instead, I unfurled my fingers and gazed down at the keyring inside my palm. Jodey's face smiled back at me from the tiny frame.

*'I don't know how you're sitting there in complete silence! No whispering, no fidgeting! You know me, Mam, I'd be losing patience by now!'*

In a break, as I went out into the foyer, the assistant coroner from the first inquest, Jo Wharton, came to wish me all the best. She had been called to give evidence at the hearing. I remembered at the first inquest she had been wearing towering bright red heels, and today, the heels were equally high, but white. It was funny, that on such a huge occasion, I was focusing on the tiny details, on the minutiae instead of the huge significance of the hearing. Perhaps it was a coping mechanism. But I like to think that it was Jodey's influence, and I could hear her commenting on every outfit, every pair of shoes.

*'Very trendy, not what I would have expected at all! How does she get around London in heels that high?'*

All that day, I sat and listened to evidence which, at times, was so brutal and heart-breaking that I had to muffle the sound of my tears with tissues. My lawyers argued that there were "multiple, significant failings" by the DWP when it terminated Jodey's ESA, and that these were not considered at the first inquest.

My barrister, Mr Nicholls said, in a written argument: "The first inquest into Ms Whiting's death provided her family with no catharsis. Indeed, the inquest has had the opposite effect given what is now known about how Ms Whiting came by her death."

The High Court heard that Jodey had received benefits for over a decade due to serious, long-term physical and mental health issues including severe pain.

Teesside and Hartlepool Coroner's Service were represented in court to respond to our claim, with the DWP allowed to make limited arguments.

Mr Nicholls said Jodey had told the DWP that she was having suicidal thoughts "a lot of the time".

In late 2016, the court was told that the DWP started to reassess Jodey, who said she needed a house visit as she was housebound, had severe anxiety and was unable to walk more than a few steps.

"There is no evidence that the department entertained that consideration at all," Mr Nicholls said.

Jodey, as I knew all too well, did not attend the assessment, and later told the DWP she had been in hospital and had not received a letter. I later found the letter at Jodey's home, but it had not been opened.

On February 6 2017, the DWP terminated her ESA, which led to both her housing benefit and council tax benefit also being terminated, the High Court heard.

Jodey was found dead in her home two weeks later. The DWP's decision to terminate the benefit was overturned only on March 31, over a month after her death.

As I sat in court, listening to the timeline leading to Jodey's suicide, it seemed just for a moment as though I was listening to someone else's story. Even though I knew each detail, each date, each gut-wrenching failure, off by heart, there was still a part of me that wondered if, this time, the ending might be different, if, this time, my daughter's life might be saved. I hoped and prayed for a last-minute intervention, I fantasised about a happy outcome. But of course it was not to be.

Mr Nicholls continued: "There is a direct link between her suicidal thoughts and her being unable to cope if her benefits were terminated... her benefits were terminated, she felt unable to cope and she killed herself, and the DWP had been told, by her, about that risk."

He argued that the department made multiple errors in handling and terminating Jodey's benefits and had even breached its own safeguarding policies.

Mr Nicholls told the High Court that it was "over-whelmingly" in the interests of justice for a fresh inquest into Jodey's death and that "the substantial truth of how Ms Whiting died was not revealed at the first inquest".

He continued: "The question of whether the termin-ation and handling of Ms Whiting's benefits and whether that caused or contributed to her death was not considered."

The barrister noted that the coroner who conducted the first inquest did not have the new evidence, including the crucial report from the independent case examiner.

Mr Nicholls said: "The up-to-date evidential picture is the one the court must consider and, in our submission, when considering that picture the court should be driven to the conclusion that there has been an insufficiency of inquiry."

It is also arguable that a different conclusion would be reached at a new inquest, the court heard.

Mr Nicholls also argued that a fresh inquest was needed to comply with the European Convention on Human

Rights, which imposes more requirements if a state body is involved. He said the DWP had provided Jodey with her income for more than 10 years and was aware of the risk to her mental health if her benefits were withdrawn.

He said in written arguments: "The DWP had assumed responsibility for Ms Whiting's welfare, they made repeated errors in the handling and termination of her ESA claim, they were aware of the significant risk if her benefits were terminated, and her suicide was a direct result of the DWP's decision.

"The DWP knew, or ought to have known, that mishandling and terminating Ms Whiting's ESA would give rise to a real and immediate risk that she would attempt suicide."

However, the coroner's service argued that it was "far from certain" that an inquest could determine whether the DWP's failings were the cause of Jodey's death.

Jonathan Hough QC, for the coroner's service, told the High Court that the coroner had called sufficient evidence to address how Jodey had died.

"It is unquestionable that the failures of DWP staff were serious and indefensible but that does not mean that the first inquest was inadequate," he said.

It was tough listening to the opposition barrister; I felt so strongly that he was wrong that it seemed like I was doing Jodey a disservice by simply sitting quietly and listening.

'Wrong, wrong, wrong!' I wanted to shout. 'I was at the first inquest, you were not!'

\* \* \*

That evening, after court had finished for the day, I gave interviews to the regional and national media. By the time I collapsed into the hotel bed, I was emotionally and physically drained. I had no energy even to flick off the bedside light. But late that night, I was woken by a dull and insistent throb in the small of my back. I made a brew using the hotel kettle and smiled as I remembered a long-ago trip to the Yorkshire seaside, when the kids were little, and we had stayed in a B&B. Donna and Jodey had been thrilled by the free sachets of tea and coffee in the rooms and they had filled a bath using all the tiny sample bottles of gel and shampoo. The result was a bath so overflowing with bubbles that nobody could get in it! They had used handfuls of the bubbles to paint each other with soapy beards and hair, whilst I took photos.

*Mam! Jodey's shoving the bubbles up my nose!*

As I drank my tea, I stared out of the hotel window at the stars twinkling in the distance, beyond the city, mere pinpricks against a dark velvet blanket of sky.

"Which is your star, Jode?" I whispered. "Send me a sign."

Knowing I had a big day ahead, I climbed back into bed, though sleep felt far away. Then, as I closed my eyes, I felt a hand slip into mine; I could even feel the soft metallic clink of her rings against my skin. It was so soothing, like a warm cardigan wrapped around me.

"Thanks, pet," I murmured, as I drifted into oblivion.

The next day, in court, we listened to more arguments, and I shed more tears. Yet I still had to pinch myself that this was really happening, that we had in fact come this far. I clutched my keyring, I remembered Jodey's hand in mine the night before, and I felt so pleased that I was doing the right thing for her. As the hearing drew to a close, representatives for the Attorney General announced that their decision would be adjourned until later in the year. I had been told this would happen but still, I felt a small stab of disappointment. As I stood up, I caught the eye of the only female judge and she seemed to form a half-smile in my direction. If not a smile, then there was certainly some compassion in her eyes. Was she a mother, like me, I wondered? Did she have a daughter? Our situations were different, doubtless, we were from different ends of the social and economic spectrums. I could not imagine that her outfit had come from a charity shop, like mine, or that she had trimmed her own fringe, with nail scissors, the day before the hearing! She was much younger than me too, and had dark, beautifully coiffured hair and subtle make-up. Yet for all the disparity, in that split-second, I felt there was an understanding and a connection between us. I returned her smile and risked a cheery wave as I made my way out.

"Mam!" Jamie whispered. "Who are you waving at?"

"Good manners cost nothing," I reminded him. "A little kindness goes a long way."

Over the next few months I would think again of the judge's smile, and the warmth in her eyes, and hope that it was a good omen.

In the meantime, we faced yet another wait and yet another rollercoaster of emotion. For me, the granting of a second inquest was the only humane and sensible decision possible. I could only trust that the High Court would agree.

We had been told to expect the decision on September 17 2021. As the date approached, I was consumed with an equal amount of excitement and trepidation. I had been warned not to get my hopes up, and by now I was used to things not going my way. And yet I felt it inconceivable, given the evidence, that we would lose.

In the few days beforehand, I had vivid dreams and in one, I was in court, before the female judge, who again smiled at me and asked me to stand before her. But the next time I looked at her, the smile had widened into a sort of sinister grimace, and she brought down a hammer on her desk with a crash.

"Take her down!" she shouted. "Lock her away. She's a drain on society!"

Frantically, as I was handcuffed, I tried to explain that I had done nothing wrong, that I was standing up for my daughter and for all the people who had no voice and no way of complaining. But it was too late. I was dragged down stone steps and into a dark space, where, through the gloom, I could just make out one of Jodey's handbags, her bright red one.

"Jodey, it's me!" I yelled. "There's been a big mix-up!"

But as we got closer, I saw the handbag was looped not over Jodey's shoulder, but over the side of a sofa. The sofa on which she had died. The stuffed monkey was there, next to the handbag, but there was no Jodey. When I awoke my arms and legs were thrashing around, as if I was trying to escape my handcuffs. I thought again about the judges, about the smile, and wondered, with a cold shudder, if my faith had been misplaced.

* * *

By the time decision day dawned, I was a bag of nerves. The announcement was not expected until 10.30am and so, before breakfast, I took the bus to the cemetery.

"It's D-day, Jode," I said. "Merry is going to call me later this morning. What are our chances? What do you think?"

The cemetery was quiet because it was so early, and there was just a hint of crispness in the air, a sure sign that autumn was on its way. So perhaps it was just the wind, whispering behind me, but I swear I felt a hand lightly brush my shoulders and my neck. And then, was that a soft voice, through the leaves?

*'Mam, you did your best. Whatever they decide, you're a winner.'*

Keen not to miss the call from my solicitor, I was back home before 10am, pacing the living room expectantly, at once willing the phone to ring yet dreading it also. By 10.45am, I could stand it no longer and I called the solicitor's London offices.

"It may take a little longer than expected," Merry's assistant explained. "I promise you will know as soon as we do."

"Of course, I'm sorry," I replied. "I'm just so wound up about this."

I waited another hour and each minute lasted at least a week. I didn't dare do any housework, in case the noise of the hoover drowned out the sound of the telephone. Then, I remembered the old adage of the watched kettle that never boils, and I decided that staring at the phone would mean it might never ring at all, so I covered it with a newspaper.

"Come on!" I fretted. "Put me out of my misery!"

I had ordered the rest of the family not to call me, so that the line was kept free. But as the morning wore on, they began sending texts and messages on Facebook.

"What's going on? What did they say?"

When, eventually, my phone rang, it split the silence like a thundercrack, and I jumped right out of the chair.

"Merry!" I gulped. "Is that you? Is it?"

There was a pause, a pause which seemed to last an eternity, a pause which seemed to stretch all the way from me to her.

"I'm sorry," she began, and in that minute, my knees gave way, and my shoulders shook with sobs.

I knew exactly what was coming. Our bid for a new inquest was lost. The three judges had dismissed the claim, finding the original inquest was sufficient. My solicitors sent me the official comments from the court and the story was soon being reported online:

'In the judgment, Mrs Justice Farbey said it would not be in the interests of justice for a new inquest, adding: "It is likely to remain a matter of speculation as to whether or not the department's decision caused Ms Whiting's suicide...

"It is not necessary and would not be in the public interest for a coroner to engage in an extensive inquiry into the department's decision-making.

"The fact that the ICE found numerous significant failings does not mean that an inquest should adduce substantial evidence about them.

"The inquest conducted by the coroner was short but fair. It covered the legal ground and dealt with the evidence before the coroner including the views of Ms Whiting's family.

"In my judgment, it would be extremely difficult for a new inquest to conclude that the department caused Ms Whiting's death."

All day, I sat on my sofa and cried. I felt as though I had been dropped from a great height, and I was emotionally bruised and badly shocked. For many days afterwards, I carried with me the bitter taste of disappointment and outrage. I knew now, with total certainty, that the system worked against the disabled, the vulnerable and the helpless. I knew now that the system worked against the very people it was supposed to protect. And that was all the motivation I needed to carry on my fight.

"What about an appeal?" my solicitor suggested, the next time we spoke. "We could apply for permission to appeal the decision of the high court?"

I had no idea how the legal system worked at all. I certainly hadn't realised we might be able to appeal. First though, it seemed, we had to apply for permission to appeal. It was such a long-winded and complex process, and no doubt was costing a fortune in legal fees. My own costs were being met by legal aid but I couldn't help worrying about the bill of tens of thousands, which would be picked up by the taxpayer. And yet this whole battle had been triggered by the removal of benefits worth £373.80. By comparison, it was a paltry amount, and it was scandalous. I did not want to rack up huge bills and I did not want a protracted legal battle. Yet I wanted to fight on – not just for Jodey, but for everyone like her.

"I'm up for it," I decided. "I'll do what it takes. How can lessons be learned, and future tragedies prevented, if no one stands up to the DWP?"

And so in October, we lodged an application for permission to appeal the High Court's judgment not to grant a second inquest into Jodey's death. We made the application for permission to appeal on several grounds including that, in light of new evidence, the court was wrong reaching its conclusion that the first inquest was sufficient to fulfil its common law duties, and that the court was wrong in deciding a fresh inquest was not necessary on the basis that the public interest does not require a broader inquiry because other forms of scrutiny exist. It was also argued that the duties under Article 2 of the Human Rights Act (the right to life) should be engaged due to the multiple serious and systematic failings of the DWP. My case was that the court was mistaken in concluding that to grant a fresh inquest it had to deem the first one insufficient. This is not the position in law, the appeal application argued.

Merry Varney gave an interview in the media when my application was launched, saying: "Our client is arguing that the Divisional Court was wrong not to find it necessary and desirable in the public interest for a second inquest to take place to investigate the possibility that DWP failings, described by the court as 'shocking', caused or contributed to Jodey's death."

# 15
# Trail Of Misery

Whilst our application was being lodged with the courts, I learned that there was to be a ground-breaking theatre production, telling the stories of people who had been failed by the DWP. The digital production, called: *Museum Of Austerity*, aimed to relay the personal stories of 10 disabled benefits claimants whose deaths between 2010-2020 have been linked publicly to the failings of the DWP. Although Jodey was not named in the production, which took the form of a mixed-reality exhibition, her story was to be told through exhibits and technology.

I was getting used to crazy and unexpected events popping up in my life, on an almost daily basis, and this was yet another one. We were invited to London to view the exhibition, which, for me, necessitated a by now familiar rush around the local charity shops to seek out a new outfit.

The exhibition, previewing at the London Film Festival, was co-produced by the English Touring Theatre, the National Theatre Storytelling Studio and Trial & Error Productions, and combined verbal testimony, including my own, with music and ground-breaking volumetric capture.

Donna, Jamie, and I attended the preview, and as we walked from room to room, reading each dark and poignant story, I could sense the agony and the helplessness that each individual must have felt. More than anything, it was so overwhelmingly sad. As we left, I spotted a poster which said the exhibition would focus on the human impact of austerity.

"Then it must focus on death," I said gloomily. "For the impact of austerity is death."

On the train home, both Jamie and I started to feel unwell and, at first, I thought that the stress of the journey and the exhibition was taking its toll. But the following day, we both tested positive for Covid, and we had to isolate. It was doubly difficult to cope with my grief when I was not allowed to visit the cemetery or to meet with my family and friends.

Luckily, we both made a full recovery but all too soon the shops were filled with Christmas displays and festive gifts, and again I was thrust back to reliving those final months before Jodey's death. Time had done nothing to ease or soften my pain, but I was learning to live with it, and that was the best I could hope for. I was slowly finding a way to be, a way to move forward in the world without my precious girl.

As December came around, we decorated her grave with photos and fairy lights and sprigs of Christmas holly. I told myself that Jodey was smiling down on us all, wearing her Christmas bauble earrings and her latest festive jumper. I wanted so much to believe it.

The week before Christmas 2021, the second documentary was aired, a Channel 4 *Dispatches* programme entitled: 'The truth about disability benefits.'

It was produced in association with Disability News Service (DNS), and John Pring, the DNS editor, who had become a close friend of mine, was an associate producer on the programme. The programme maker was Richard Butchins, who himself had a disability and a valid personal insight and contribution. I had got to know Richard too, over a series of interviews, and I had so much admiration for them both.

That evening, we gathered at Jamie's flat to watch the programme. One gaping absence was my good friend, Jan, who had been with me through the early part of my campaign. Jan had died in her sleep in May 2020, aged 65, after a long battle against health problems including chronic obstructive pulmonary disease. I missed her dreadfully, but I knew she would be proud of the programme.

Even though I was used to seeing Jodey's face on TV, my stomach was still churning with butterflies as the opening scene was shown. I just wanted it to go well, and more than anything, I didn't want to let her down. And there were tens of thousands of people now following and supporting our campaign, so I had a duty to make them proud too. Hearing my own voice, coming from the TV, was strange and I cringed a little. And then, when I saw Jodey's photo, I started to cry.

In the film, Richard said that he could not find any data on suicide and benefits – a shocking fact in itself – so he had collected his own, designing a survey in conjunction with the Centre for Welfare Reform. The survey was sent to 80,000 claimants and of the 3,500 who responded, 13 per cent said they had attempted suicide as a result of interacting with the DWP. A third said it had caused them to plan suicide, while 61 per cent said the way the system is implemented led them to have suicidal thoughts. The statistics were appalling, but they were hardly surprising.

The survey found that:

- 89 per cent of respondents said the DWP is not "an ally to disabled people" as it claims to be.
- 96 per cent found the preparation for their assessment distressing.
- 93 per cent said the process of claiming benefits had made their mental health worse.
- 89 per cent said it had aggravated their pre-existing conditions.
- 79 per cent said it had made their physical health worse.
- 61 per cent said it had caused them new health problems.

Richard said: "What it tells us is that there are a lot more people out there killing themselves and attempting to kill themselves by the way this system is implemented than is officially acknowledged.

"These figures point to an underlying disregard for people's lives, which I find really disturbing."

Richard explained that he first became aware in 2008 of "a sort of continual background rumble of serious harms" when ESA and its eligibility test – the Work Capability Assessment – were introduced for people with disabilities or long-term health conditions making new claims. The DWP had begun the process of reassessing all claimants in 2011. He said he would equate the current system "in a way to the Windrush hostile environment".

He said: "They have set it up so they're looking for reasons not to give you the money that you're entitled to. It feels like you have to humiliate yourself to get this money from the Government."

But despite 82 deaths linked to benefits being reported in the media between 2008 and 2020, he said he was not surprised the story has not had its "Windrush moment".

He said: "There should have been a national scandal on several occasions, frankly. But there hasn't because society sees disability as an individual tragedy. Racism is seen as a societal issue, but it barely even registers on people's brains that there could be such a thing as ableism."

He also said he thought people are reluctant to engage with the issue "because it frightens them, it makes them aware of their own frailty".

As well as my own contribution, the film included interviews with the family members of three other deceased claimants.

Errol Graham, 57, who had a history of mental health problems, starved to death in his Nottingham flat after his benefits were stopped. He weighed four-and-a-half stone when bailiffs found his body.

The inquest into the death of 27-year-old mother, Philippa Day, who had been diagnosed with unstable personality disorder, found 28 errors in the management of her benefit claim by both the DWP and private contractor Capita. Her family was told that if she did not attend her assessment, when she was in a coma, her application would be cancelled. The coroner found the failures were the "predominant factor" in her overdose.

Roy Curtis, 27, who was autistic, took his own life six days after being told to attend a "fitness for work" assessment, despite the DWP being repeatedly warned its actions had made him suicidal. His body lay undiscovered in his flat for nine months.

I had heard their stories before, I had met these families, I had wept with them. Even so, to hear their tragedies, spelled out so plainly and so publicly, was gut-twisting. I felt Jamie's arms around me as my whole body was racked with cries.

The documentary went on to say that between 2012 and 2021, the DWP had conducted 268 secret reviews about claimants who had come to serious harm. They were not routinely published, and bereaved families were not routinely informed when they began. In 2020, the programme said, the DWP admitted it had shredded 50 reviews into suicides linked to benefits being stopped.

A whistle-blower inside the DWP told the programme "the customers are viewed with contempt" and "mental health was certainly an area that staff used to joke about".

Shockingly, the comment was not a shock to me.

Richard said: "The cracks are really wide. People are still falling through them at a rate that I think is really unacceptable."

Although his own application for Personal Independence Payment was "reasonably straightforward", he said he still needed someone to help him fill in the 30-page form. And he admitted to being "overwhelmed by anxiety" at the prospect of having to be reassessed again in two years.

He said: "It feels to me like the DWP is using process as punishment and that should stop."

In the film Richard also called for an end to the regular reassessment of claimants with a lifelong condition, the removal of private contractors and their profit motive from the system, a shortening of the lengthy forms and a scrapping of most assessments in favour of gathering evidence from an individual's doctor.

He said: "What I would like to see is people not being terrified of applying for a benefit."

His words struck a resounding chord within me. He had summed it up perfectly.

But he admitted: "Until non-disabled people take up the torch, it's not going to change."

A spokesperson for the DWP told the programme: "Our sincere condolences remain with the families of Philippa, Errol, Jodey and Roy. We support millions of people every year. Our priority is they get the benefits to which they are entitled as soon as possible, and to ensure they receive a supportive and compassionate service. This happens in the vast majority of cases but when sadly this does not, we take it very seriously and identify any lessons learned."

After the programme ended, we remembered Jodey together, with a fish and chip supper. I could not stop thinking about the other three people on the programme too and how they had suffered, all alone. And the reaction to the programme on social media reflected yet more wide-reaching despair:

One disabled claimant said on Twitter: "I attempted suicide in October 2017 due to the DWP. I was refused benefits and it took four years to get to Tribunal where I won."

Another, after watching the programme, said the system was "unnecessarily cruel and inhuman", and described how the written report produced by the healthcare professional who had assessed them had been "a work of fiction".

And another said: "I have been subject to these dehumanising, degrading processes. Then the lies that follow in the reports. It's cruelty.

"As someone who worked in safeguarding prior to losing my job through health, I don't know how they can behave as they do."

\* \* \*

Dolly Sen's documentary, *Broken Hearts for the DWP, Who's Paying the Rent to your Heart*, was also streamed in December 2021. The film revolved around art interventions designed by Dolly and her team, including the broken hearts protest outside the DWP.

The documentary, which went on to become a multiple film festival winner, looked at how the DWP is driving disabled people to starvation and suicide and how disabled people are fighting back using art, love and…rage!

In the film, Dolly explained how she had written to the government asking them not to break any more hearts through the workings of the DWP, and that the Prime Minister had failed to reply. In the absence of a response, Dolly staged an intervention at Caxton House, head office of the DWP, which I was a very proud part of. After the programme was released, the actress Maxine Peake said on Twitter:

"Dolly's film is one of the most important films I have seen in a long time. Urgent, powerful, devastating. We all need to act."

It was high praise from an actress I had huge respect for. I only hoped that her comments would make people sit up and take notice.

In February 2022, a report that the DWP had initially refused to publish was released, and it found that some disabled benefits claimants cannot afford to buy food or pay for heating. The government had kept the 80-page report secret for over a year, until a committee of MPs demanded that it was published. The report found for claimants, benefits "offered a regular income which provided reassurance that some of their essential day-to-day living costs would be met".

But some of the poorest "were often unable to meet essential day-to-day living needs, such as heating their house or buying food". The report also highlighted some of the poorest claimants – in low-paid jobs, with unmanageable debt, or out-of-work households – whose only income came from the welfare system.

It added: "Those with children who had restricted financial resources usually described putting their own needs, including their health-related needs, after those of their children.

"These poorer benefit claimants with children were sometimes led to limit or stop spending on their health.

It went on: "Decisions about what to spend limited financial resources on were unique to each individual's particular health and personal circumstances, with participants weighing up and prioritising spending on different needs.

"As a result, some additional needs were not met, such as transport costs for healthcare appointments, additional therapies, equipment and aids and in-home adaptations.

"In these circumstances participants either went without or saved up to afford these costs occasionally or rationing their usage."

Some "borrowed from family and friends" or "used support services such as food banks", the report added.

The report, 'Uses of Health and Disability Benefits', was based on "in-depth interviews" with 120 long-term sick or disabled people and sent to the government in September 2020. The Commons Work and Pensions Committee, which finally obtained and published it over a year later, said DWP Secretary Therese Coffey repeatedly refused to publish it.

Chairman Stephen Timms said: "The report gives a valuable insight into the experiences of people claiming health and disability benefits.

"While the system is working for some, we now know that others reported that they are still unable to meet essential living costs such as food and utility bills."

Reading the report, I was bombarded with unhappy memories of Jodey, unable to afford heating, huddled in her hat and gloves under a quilt or unable to buy food, nibbling on toast without butter. I remembered my humbling trip to the food bank on her behalf and my last futile and humiliating appeal to the Job Centre. Our own tragedy was all-consuming. And yet, it was not the only one. The report, and the subsequent and cowardly delay in publication, made my blood boil.

*'Don't let them get away with it, Mam. Change has to come. And you can be the one to bring it.'*

# 16
# Jodey's Legacy

It is March 2022, and still we have heard nothing from the High Court following our application for permission to appeal the decision not to grant a second inquest for Jodey. Each morning, I whisper a silent prayer, hoping that good news might be just a phone call away. The wait is frustrating and yet I have a belief, backed up by no logic whatsoever, that the long delay is a good sign for us.

In the meantime, Justice For Jodey is going strong. I have recently given interviews to Channel 5 and to my own regional channels, and taken part in a parliamentary debate alongside the Shadow Work and Pensions Secretary, Jonathan Ashworth. He, like me, is pushing for an independent public inquiry into deaths linked to the actions of the DWP.

Mr Ashworth said: "We definitely should have a proper inquiry. It seems to me entirely right that we need to change the system so these awful, most tragic events do not happen again.

"If I was Secretary of State for Work and Pensions then a proper inquiry into these matters would be something that I would definitely want to pursue."

# A Mother's Job

My local paper, the *Gazette*, has remained loyal and reliable and they support every new development in our fight. I am so grateful to the reporters and the lawyers, and most of all to my family and friends, who have helped the campaign to get this far.

This coming year, again with my family's help, I would like to set up a charity offering practical help to others, specifically providing grief counselling for children and advice with planning funerals and negotiating the system which, as we know to our cost, is a complete minefield. Jodey loved children and so we would like the focus of the charity to be on young people.

And, though it is just a pipedream, I would one day love to open a drop-in café for people with mental health issues. I have dreamed many times of a cosy little place, on the high street, with Jodey's name lit up above the door; a beacon for people who, like her, feel that they have nowhere else to turn. I would like those people to know that they can turn to me.

My family continues to make me immeasurably proud. Donna's own two children are grown up now and she is a grandmother of four. Jamie runs a carpet-cleaning business, and he has a teenage daughter. Jodey's children miss her just as much as I do, but they also know that life is precious, and that their own must go on. To date, I have 14 grandchildren, 16 great grand-children – and counting! I am blessed.

Each night, I light a candle for Jodey at her little shrine in my home and each weekend, I visit her grave. When I am at my lowest, I spray her Right Guard and I wear her cream jumper, and if I close my eyes, I can often feel her hand in mine. Sometimes, I hear her giggling or cursing her two budgies. She has not left me, not completely, and it is my belief that she never will. The bond between a mother and a child is strong enough to survive everything, even death.

A little over five years ago, I was an ordinary mother and grandmother. There was nothing more pressing in my life than getting to the bus stop in the rain or picking up a bag of Rainbow Drops for Jodey. I believed, like any mother, that my disabled daughter would be supported and assisted by our society. I never dreamed that, at her very lowest, she would be kicked aside to die alone.

I have to believe that Jodey died for a reason, and that her death can bring about change and progress. My tragedy has transformed me from the passive and easygoing person I used to be. I am a fighter and a battler, and I can hold my own with politicians and judges and journalists. Every day, I curse my own previous naivety, my misplaced faith in a broken system, and, in Jodey's memory, I want to help fix it. I want her name to be synonymous with justice. There will always be an enduring sadness inside me, and I will never recover from losing the daughter I love so dearly. But sitting alongside my grief there is a growing feeling of pride and of triumph, that her legacy lives on.

# Other bestselling Mirror Books

## The Convent
### *Marie Hargreaves*

*With Ann and Joe Cusack*

**When a fancy car pulls up outside six-year-old Marie's home in Oldham, in 1959, she is told she is going on holiday...**

In fact, she is taken to live in a convent, overseen by a cruel and sadistic nun. There, a horrific ritual of physical, sexual and mental abuse begins.

Marie feels unable to share details of her suffering with anyone. Until years later, when a police investigation is launched, and she realises that the time has finally come to tell the truth...

# written by Ann and Joe Cusack

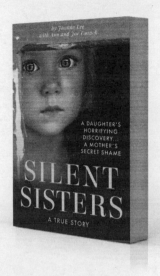

## Silent Sisters

### *Joanne Lee*

*With Ann and Joe Cusack*

**A DEADLY SECRET. A HORRIFYING DISCOVERY.**

**For over 20 years, Joanne Lee's mother kept the remains of her newborn babies hidden in her wardrobe.**

Growing up in a chaotic Merseyside household, Joanne suffered neglect and abusive control while her mother lapsed into a downward spiral. But the consequences of her mother's messy lifestyle turned out to be far worse than Joanne could ever have imagined – the family home held a sinister secret.

In Silent Sisters, Joanne, who was falsely accused of murdering her own baby sister, tells her story for the first time – her struggle to piece together the truth and to give four babies the proper burial they deserve.

MIRROR BOOKS

# Other bestselling Mirror Books

## The Asylum
*Carol Minto*

*With Ann and Joe Cusack*

**Born into poverty and with mostly absent parents, Carol helped to raise her nine siblings. But when she was just 11 years old, her older brother began to sexually abuse her.**

After four years, Carol managed to escape – and ran away from home. Picked up by social services they placed her at the infamous Aston Hall psychiatric hospital in Derby where she was stripped, sedated, assaulted and raped by the doctor in charge.

This is the full story of how she overcame unimaginable suffering, to find the solace she has today as a mother and grandmother.

# written by Ann and Joe Cusack

# The Boy With A Pound In His Pocket

*Jade Akoum*

*With Ann and Joe Cusack*

**Yousef Makki was stabbed in the heart by one of his friends on a quiet, leafy street in the wealthy Manchester suburb of Hale Barns.**

Just four months after he was killed, a jury found his friend not guilty of murder or manslaughter. Yousef died from a single stab wound to the chest. When his sister, Jade, collected his blood-stained clothes, he had a single pound coin in his pocket. This is Jade's moving, personal story of how the fight for justice has transformed her life.

MIRROR BOOKS